MODERN HISTORY

MODERN HISTORY

PETER
BEDRICK
BOOKS

This edition published in 2002 by Peter Bedrick Books
an imprint of McGraw-Hill Children's Publishing
8787 Orion Place
Columbus, OH 43240

The material in this book has previously appeared in
History of the World (Bounty, Octopus Publishing Group Ltd, 2001)

ISBN 1-57768-955-0

Printed in China

McGraw-Hill
Children's Publishing

A Division of The ***McGraw-Hill*** *Companies*

PHOTOGRAPHIC CREDITS

6 (B/L) Leonard de Selva/CORBIS; 8 (C) Hulton-Deutsch Collection/CORBIS; 10 (B) Bettmann/CORBIS; 13 (T/R) Sean Sexton Collection/CORBIS; 14 (B) CORBIS; 17 (T/R) Archivo Iconografico, S.A./CORBIS; 18 (C) CORBIS; 26 (B/R) Hulton-Deutsch Collection/CORBIS; 32 (B/L) Bettmann/CORBIS; 33 (T/R) Tim Page/CORBIS; 36 (C) Bettmann/CORBIS; 37 (T/R) National Archives and Records Administration; 38 (B/R) Bettmann/CORBIS; 39 (B/R) reproduced courtesy of Nokia; 41 (T/R) AFP/CORBIS; 43 (T/L) reproduced courtesy of Greenpeace;
45 (B/L) Arne Hodalic/CORBIS, (T/R) reproduced courtesy of NASA. All other images from the Miles Kelly Archive.

QUOTATION ACKNOWLEDGMENTS

Pages 13, 19 and 31 published in the *Oxford Dictionary of Quotations* by the Oxford University Press; page 37 quoted in *World Book Encyclopedia*, published by World Book, Inc.; pages 9, 23 and 41 quoted in *The Norton Anthology of Poetry*, published by W. W. Norton and Co.

Every effort has been made to trace all copyright holders and obtain permissions. The editor and publishers sincerely apologize for any inadvertent errors or omissions and will be happy to correct them in any future editions.

Contents

AUSTRALIA The First Fleet 36c
May 1787 · Departure
AUSTRALIA The First Fleet 36c
May 1787 · Departure
AUSTRALIA The First Fleet 36c
May 1787 · Departure
AUSTRALIA The First Fleet 36c
May 1787 · Departure

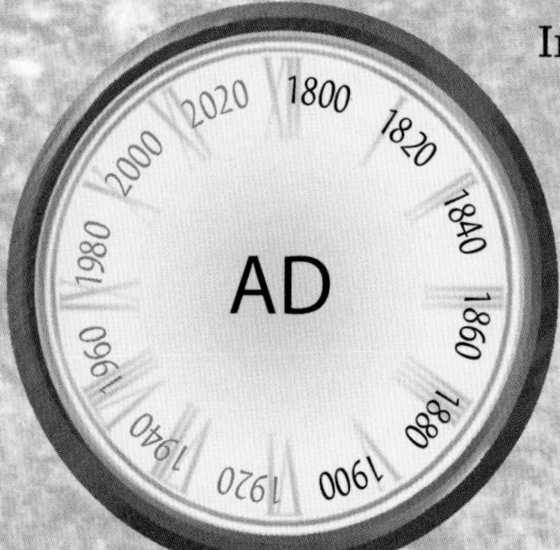

In April 1770, Captain James Cook had sailed along the east coast of Australia. He and his crew had landed at a place they called "Botany Bay" and claimed the land for Britain, naming the region New South Wales.

Colonies in Australia

First Fleet arrives in Botany Bay.	1788
Van Diemen's Land (Tasmania) settled.	1801
Assisted migration scheme introduced. Free settlers start to arrive in Australia.	1831
Gold discovered in Australia triggering a gold rush.	1851
Bush ranging comes to an end with execution of Ned Kelly.	1880
Economic depression in Australia.	1890
Commonwealth of Australia proclaimed (January 1).	1901

Eighteen years later, in 1788, the first ships full of settlers arrived from Britain. These settlers were all convicts, transported from Britain for their various crimes. Under the command of Captain Arthur Phillip, the convicts were set to work founding a penal colony in Botany Bay.

Convicts and settlers

As more convicts arrived, the colony grew. When a convict's sentence was over, or if a convict was pardoned, he or she became free and was known as an "emancipist." Many emancipists stayed in the colony and made new lives for themselves. From the 1830s onward, an increasing number of free settlers also began to arrive in New South Wales, attracted by promises of grants of land. By the early 1850s, four new Australian colonies had been established: Western Australia, South Australia, Victoria, and Tasmania. The transportation of convicts ended in the 1840s and 1850s.

The Aborigines

The arrival of European settlers had a devastating effect on the original inhabitants of Australia, the Aborigines. The Europeans introduced diseases unknown to the Aborigines, to which they had no natural resistance. Many Aborgines were killed by outbreaks of diseases such as smallpox. As the number of colonists increased, forcing the Aborigines

△ *A set of modern Australian stamps commemorates the arrival of the First Fleet in Botany Bay in January 1788. The fleet consisted of 11 ships of convicts, army officers, and soldiers.*

△ *About 300,000 Aborigines were living in Australia when the settlers first arrived from Europe. They were divided into about 500 tribal groups.*

Gold mining

Gold was discovered in New South Wales and Victoria in 1851. The find immediately attracted thousands of gold seekers from European countries and from China. Although a few prospectors grew rich, many found nothing and, unable to pay their passage home, settled in Australia.

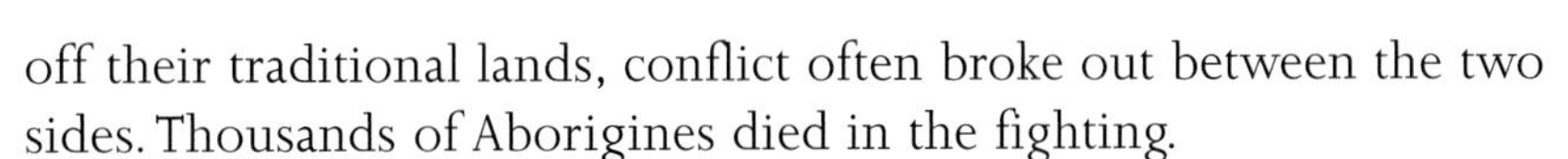

off their traditional lands, conflict often broke out between the two sides. Thousands of Aborigines died in the fighting.

European exploration of the Australian continent continued in the 1800s. In 1840–1841, Edward Eyre became the first European to cross the Nullarbor Plain in south Australia. In 1861–1862 John Stuart made a successful journey northward across the Simpson Desert.

△ *This carved club (left) and parry stick (right) are traditional Aboriginal weapons. The Aborigines' wooden clubs and spears were no match for the guns of the European settlers.*

A new nation

By the 1880s, there were seven independent colonies in Australia. The introduction of the telegraph and construction of the railways improved links between the colonies, and a new movement started to join the colonies together in a federation. On January 1, 1901, the Commonwealth of Australia was created. Edmund Barton became the first prime minister of the new federal government. At that time, many people in Australia believed that only white people should be allowed into their new country. A "White Australia" policy was introduced to prevent Asian immigration into Australia. This policy was to last for more than 70 years.

At the beginning of World War I, both Australia and New Zealand sent troops to join the fighting. The Australia and New Zealand Army Corps – the Anzacs – took part in the disastrous campaign in Gallipoli, Turkey, establishing a brave fighting reputation. Many Anzac troops also fought in the trenches along the Western Fron

◁ ***Convicts were to be transported to Australia and confined in prison ships like this one, until the late 1860s. Around 160,000 convicts were sent to Australia over an 80 year period.***

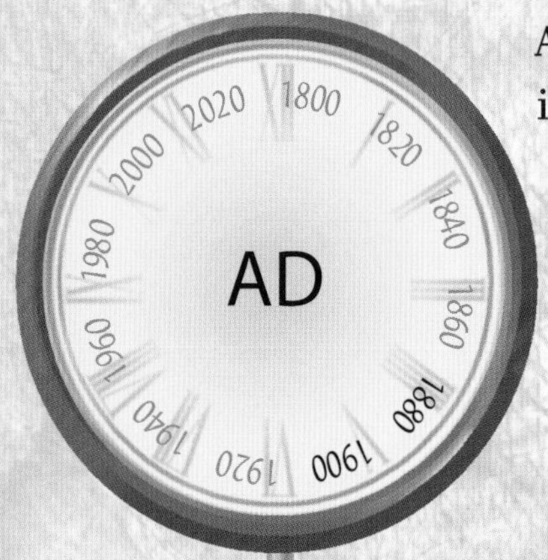

As the 19th century drew to a close, there was an increase in rivalry between the different nations of Europe. They competed against each other for control of colonies, and for industrial and military power.

World War I Begins

In 1882, Germany, Austria-Hungary and Italy (known as the Central Powers) formed an alliance, called the Triple Alliance, promising to protect each other in the event of an attack. In 1904, Britain joined with France in a similar alliance. They were joined by Russia in 1907 to form the Triple Entente.

Germany, Austria-Hungary, and Italy form Triple Alliance.	1882
Germany develops naval force to rival Britain's navy.	1898
Britain and France agree Entente Cordiale.	1904
Russia joins Britain and France to form Triple Entente.	1907
Austria-Hungary adds Bosnia and Herzegovina to its empire.	1908
June: Archduke Ferdinand shot in Sarajevo.	1914
July: Austria-Hungary declares war on Serbia.	1914
August: Austria-Hungary invades Russia. Germany invades Belgium and France.	1914
September: German advance halted by Allies.	1914

Events in Sarajevo

Europe was finally plunged into war by the action of an assassin in the Bosnian city of Sarajevo in 1914. Since 1908, Bosnia had been part of the Austro-Hungarian Empire, but many people in Bosnia were Serbs, who wanted to be part of neighboring Serbia.

In June 1914, the heir to the Austro-Hungarian throne, Archduke Franz Ferdinand, and his wife Sophie made a tour of Bosnia. As they drove through the streets of Sarajevo, a Serbian assassin shot them both dead. In retaliation, Austria-Hungary, backed by Germany, declared war on Serbia.

Soon all the major European powers were drawn into the conflict. Russia, backed by France, supported Serbia. Then Germany invaded neutral Belgium and attacked France, drawing Britain into the conflict.

△ German soldiers in trenches along the Western Front. During the four years of the war, many thousands of soldiers were to die in the trenches as they battled to gain a few yards, or miles, of ground. On the command of their officers, soldiers would climb "over the top" and run across "no man's land" while firing at the soldiers in the enemy trenches.

△ *A British soldier from World War I. Typically, soldiers would spend a week or more in a front-line trench before going back to their dugout in a support trench.*

Shooting in Sarajevo

The assassination of Archduke Ferdinand and his wife took place shortly after this photograph was taken. As they drove around Sarajevo, the assassin leapt onto the car and fired two shots.

The Western and Eastern fronts

The war was fought in two main areas in Europe, known as the Western Front and the Eastern Front. In September 1914, the Allies (France and Britain) managed to halt the German advance toward Paris at the first battle of the Marne. But after this crucial victory, the Germans and the Allies reached a kind of stalemate in which neither side could make any ground. Their troops dug themselves into zigzag lines of defensive trenches, which eventually stretched from the English Channel almost to Switzerland. This was known as the Western Front.

The Eastern Front ran along the borders between Russia and its Central Power enemies of Germany and Austria-Hungary. Despite having a huge army, the Russians were badly equipped, and they suffered heavy defeats at the battles of Tannenberg and the Masurian Lakes in 1914. However, further south Russian forces had more success against the Austro-Hungarian forces in Galicia, gaining territory that was subsequently lost again in 1915. After the Russian Revolution in 1917, the new government withdrew Russia from the war.

> "If I should die, think only this of me;
> That there's some corner of a foreign field
> That is for ever England.
>
> *THE SOLDIER*, RUPERT BROOKE
>
> *Brooke was a poet who was killed in 1915. He was 28 when he died.*"

△ *A World War I gas mask. After the Germans used poisonous gas for the first time in April 1915, masks became an essential part of every soldier's kit.*

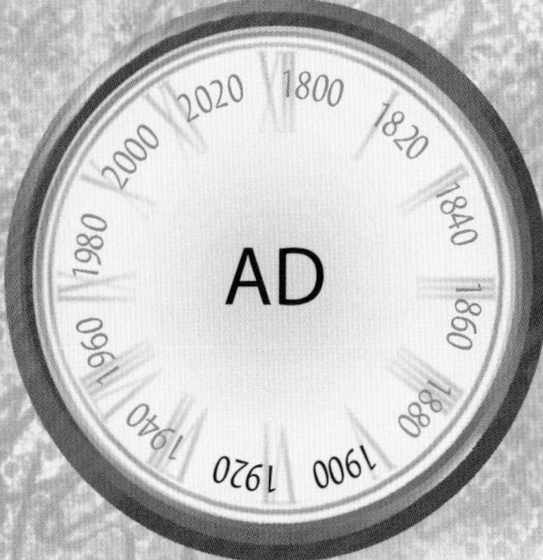

Before the war, Germany had built up its navy to match the strength of the British navy. However, the battle of Jutland in 1916 was the only major sea battle between the two navies during World War I, and Britain managed to maintain control of the seas throughout the war.

The Great War

From the start of the Great War, the name by which World War I was first known, British warships blockaded German ports. In this way Britain's navy prevented supplies from reaching Germany, causing severe shortages of food and other goods. The Germans retaliated with their submarines, called U-boats. After 1915, U-boats attacked both warships and merchant shipping carrying supplies to Britain.

Allies land in Gallipoli. Italy declares war on Austria-Hungary. — 1915

February: battle of Verdun. May: sea battle of Jutland. July: battle of the Somme. — 1916

April: U.S. declares war on Germany. June: U.S. troops arrive in France. — 1917

Battle of Passchendaele. Revolution in Russia. End of fighting on Eastern Front. — 1917

President Woodrow gives "14 Points" for peace. Last battles on Western Front. — 1918

Germans sign armistice on November 11. — 1918

Paris Peace Conference. — 1919

In May 1915, a German torpedo hit a British passenger ship called the *Lusitania*. The ship was carrying nearly 2,000 passengers, including many Americans. The sinking of the *Lusitania* was one of the factors that eventually drew the United States into the war.

△ *The surprise torpedo attack of the Lusitania took place off the Irish coast. The U-boats fired powerful torpedoes which exploded when they struck a ship traveling on the surface.*

△ The battle of the Somme took place in northern France in 1916. It lasted for about five months, during which time over one million soldiers were killed.

Peace treaty

The Allies and Germany signed the Treaty of Versailles on June 28, 1919 in Paris. The date was the fifth anniversary of the shooting of Archduke Ferdinand in Sarajevo.

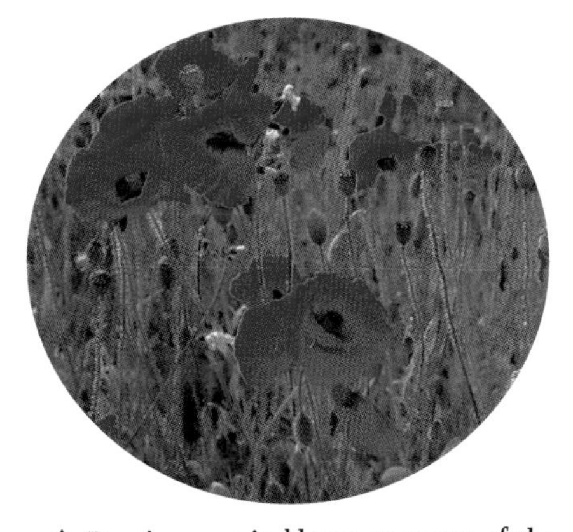

△ Poppies were in bloom on many of the French battlefields of World War I. Today, artificial poppies are sold in Europe and the U.S. to raise money for war veterans.

War on other fronts

During 1915 and 1916 the war spread to other regions. Italy entered the war on the side of the Allies in 1915, and Italian troops fought Austro-Hungarian forces in the Alpine regions along the border between the two countries.

In April 1915, the Allies attacked Turkey (which had joined the Central Powers in 1914) with the aim of capturing its capital, Constantinople. Allied troops, including many soldiers from Australia and New Zealand, were sent to the Gallipoli Peninsula on the coast of the Dardanelles. However, the attack was a failure and the Allies were forced to withdraw. Allied troops also fought Turkish forces in the Middle East, in a successful attempt to keep control of the vital supply link of the Suez Canal.

The end

On the Western Front, the deadlock continued. Battles such as the Somme offensive in 1916, and Passchendaele in 1917, achieved little and caused the deaths of thousands of soldiers. However, in April 1917 the U.S. joined World War I, boosting the Allies with new supplies of troops. Although Germany launched a fresh attack on the Western Front in 1918, by late September it was clear that the Central Powers were defeated.

△ Battles between enemy aircraft were known as "dogfights." The Germans' invention of a machine gun that fired rounds between the plane's propeller blades made this combat more dangerous.

The Paris Peace Conference

On November 9, Kaiser Wilhelm II, the German ruler, was forced to abdicate. On November 11, 1918 an armistice, or peace agreement, was signed and the war was over. At the Paris Peace Conference, held in 1919, Germany was held responsible for the war and forced to pay large amounts of reparations (compensation) to its former enemies.

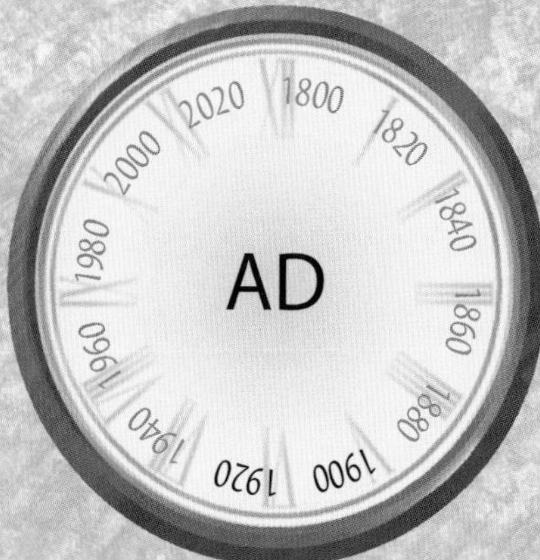

During World War I, the issue of Home Rule continued to cause conflict in Ireland. The third Home Rule Bill had been passed by the British parliament in 1914, but the outbreak of war in the same year delayed the start of Home Rule.

Home Rule in Ireland

Third Home Rule bill passed by British parliament but held up by outbreak of war.	1914
Easter Rebellion in Dublin.	1916
Sinn Fein declares itself in favor of an Irish republic.	1917
Sinn Fein sets up Irish parliament, Dáil Eirann. Fighting breaks out.	1919
British parliament passes Government of Ireland Act, dividing country into two.	1920
Truce stops fighting. Anglo-Irish Treaty splits Sinn Fein.	1921
Civil war breaks out between supporters of treaty and those against it.	1922
Republicans, led by de Valera, accept Anglo-Irish Treaty.	1923

Many people in Ireland supported Home Rule because they believed that Ireland should have its own parliament in Dublin and control its own affairs. These nationalists were mostly Irish Catholics in the south of the country. They formed various organizations, including the political party Sinn Fein and the armed force of the Irish Volunteers.

Irish Protestants, however, were bitterly opposed to Home Rule. They were in the majority in the northern province of Ulster, and believed that they would be treated unfairly by a Dublin parliament. They formed the Ulster Volunteer Force to protect themselves if Home Rule was introduced.

The Easter Rising

When war broke out in 1914, most Irish Volunteers supported Britain in its fight against the Central Powers. But a breakaway group formed the Irish Republican Brotherhood (later known as the IRA). On Easter Monday 1916, protestors belonging to this and other nationalist movements seized buildings in Dublin and proclaimed Ireland a republic. British troops bombarded the rebels for a week until they surrendered.

△ The rebellion of Easter Monday 1916 became known as the Easter Rising. Many Irish people were unhappy about the heavy-handed tactics of the British soldiers, and the rebels soon became public heroes.

△ The British prime minister, David Lloyd George, met five representatives from the *Dáil* in London in 1921. Under his proposal, Northern Ireland would stay under British control but the Irish Free State would become a British dominion.

Michael Collins

Michael Collins was one of the leaders of the Irish Republican Army (IRA) who supported the 1922 Anglo-Irish Treaty. The peace treaty split the IRA in two. The bitter civil war between opponents and supporters of the treaty continued until a ceasefire was accepted in 1923.

Fifteen of the republican leaders were executed for their part in the uprising. One of the leaders, Eamon de Valera, was sentenced to death and then later reprieved.

The Anglo-Irish Treaty

In 1917, the political party Sinn Fein backed forming an Irish republic. The next year, the party won 73 seats in the general election. Sinn Fein's MPs formed their own parliament, the *Dáil Eirann*, in Dublin and in 1919 declared Ireland a republic. There followed three years of bitter fighting between the IRA and the Royal Irish Constabulary, backed by British troops known as "black and tans" because of the color of their uniforms.

In July 1921, a truce was declared and the fighting stopped. Lloyd George, Britain's prime minister, proposed that the country should be divided into Northern Ireland, made up of six counties of the northeast, and the Irish Free State, made up of the 26 counties of the south. The *Dáil* approved the Anglo-Irish Treaty in 1921. Fighting broke out between Republicans wanting a united, independent Ireland, and the Free Staters who supported the treaty. It ended in 1923 when de Valera's Republicans accepted the treaty.

△ Ireland's flag was first used in the 1800s. Its green color stands for the Roman Catholic population, the white is for unity and the orange color stands for the Protestant people of Ulster.

"Before Irish Home Rule is conceded by the Imperial Parliament, England ... will have to be convinced of its justice and equity.

LORD ROSEBERY, HOUSE OF LORDS, MARCH 1894

Rosebery favored social reform. He was Prime Minister from 1894–1895."

The end of World War I left devastation across large areas of Europe. Many countries were in economic chaos too. Germany was struggling to pay reparations to its former enemies. Countries such as France and Britain had borrowed large amounts of money to pay for the war effort, mostly from banks in the United States.

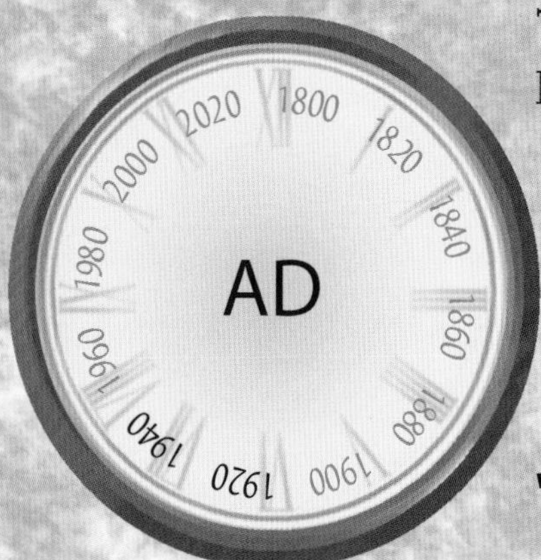

The Great Depression

The Great Depression started in 1929 in the United States, and continued for about ten years. It was a time of high unemployment and great poverty. Although the Depression began in the U.S., it quickly became a worldwide phenomenon that affected millions of people.

Panic selling of shares leads to the Wall Street Crash.	1929
Share prices continue to fall for following three years.	1930s
Drought and dust storms devastate the Midwest and southwest regions of the U.S.	1930s
Franklin D. Roosevelt becomes president and sets up the "New Deal."	1932
Outbreak of war brings an end to the Depression.	1939
John Steinbeck's The Grapes of Wrath tells about migrant families.	1939
Full employment returns in the United States.	1941

The Wall Street Crash

In the late 1920s, the price of shares on the New York Stock Exchange increased rapidly. More and more people bought stocks and shares in the hope of selling them again when their price had gone up – therefore making a large profit. When prices dropped in October 1929, people rushed to sell their stocks and shares before it was too late, but prices fell even further. This event is known as the Wall Street Crash. Thousands of

△ In October 1929 prices on New York's Stock Exchange began to collapse. This is the Stock Exchange at the time, with brokers spilling out onto the streets of the city.

△ In 1932 Franklin D. Roosevelt was elected president. His "New Deal" aimed to create jobs and to protect people's savings by regulating banks more closely.

△ During the worst years of the Depression, many people were forced to rely on charity and government hand outs for their most basic needs.

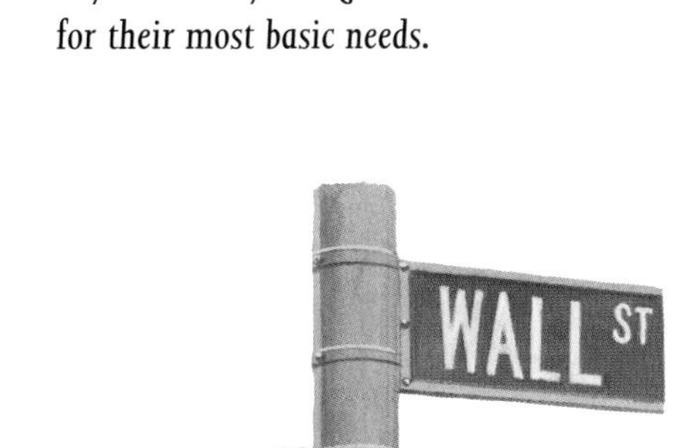

△ Wall Street lies at the heart of New York's business and banking district. Many banks have offices in the narrow street. The name "Wall Street" is a worldwide symbol for financial business.

people lost all their money, many businesses and banks shut down and unemployment soared.

The situation in the U.S. was made worse by severe droughts in the 1930s in the Midwest states. Thousands of farm workers were ruined. Many made the long and difficult journey to look for work on farms in California. Thousands died from disease and hunger.

Depression in Europe

The economic collapse in the United States had a drastic effect on countries around the world. Banks in the U.S. withdrew funds from overseas and demanded the repayment of loans, triggering the closure of many European banks. Many European countries tried to protect their own trade by raising taxes on imports, but this encouraged a worldwide slump in international trade. Both Great Britain and Germany were very badly affected by the Great Depression. In Germany, Adolf Hitler rose to power in the 1930s, promising the suffering German people to make their country proud and strong once again.

A New Deal

In 1933, President Franklin D. Roosevelt introduced a program to help the needy, to create jobs, and to help struggling farmers. It was known as the "New Deal." But it was the onset of war that finally ended the Great Depression in both the U.S. and Europe. As countries such as Britain and Germany prepared for the possibility of war, the production of munitions and armaments soared, creating many jobs. And with the outbreak of war in 1939, orders flooded into factories on both sides of the Atlantic Ocean.

Jarrow march

In 1935, a group of 200 unemployed workers from Britain's northern industrial cities marched from Jarrow to London to draw attention to their plight.

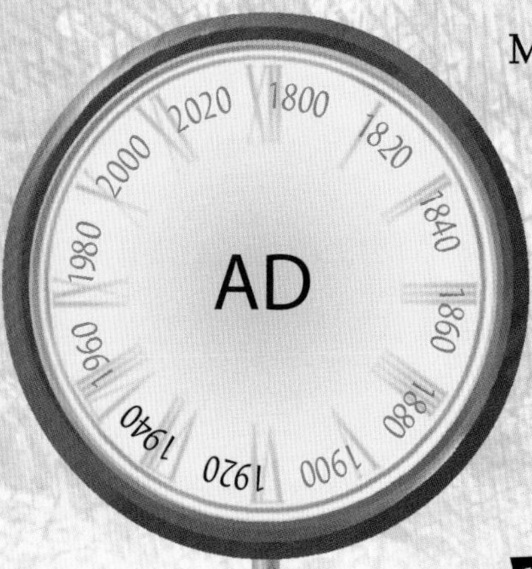

Many people hoped that World War I was the "war to end all wars." But the settlements drawn up in 1919 provided the starting-point for a whole new set of problems. In addition, the misery and suffering brought by the Great Depression during the 1920s and 1930s led to political changes in many countries.

The Dictators

Benito Mussolini marches to Rome.	1922
Mussolini becomes dictator of Italy, known as il Duce.	1925
Sir Oswald Mosley sets up British Union of Fascists.	1932
Nazis come to power in Germany, led by Adolf Hitler.	1933
"Night of the Long Knives" in Germany as Hitler eliminates his rivals.	1934
Spanish Civil War.	1936–1939
Germany annexes Austria and the Sudetenland.	1938
General Franco becomes dictator of Spain.	1939

In Europe, all these factors led to the growth of the Fascist movement. The word "Fascism" comes from *fasces*, meaning a bundle of branches. It was the symbol of authority in ancient Rome. Fascism promised strong leadership and to restore the national economy and pride. This was a very powerful message in the years of the Great Depression, and many people in Europe supported the various Fascist parties.

Fascism in Italy

Italy was the first country to have a Fascist ruler. In 1922, Benito Mussolini marched to Rome and demanded that the Italian king, Victor Emmanuel III, make him prime minister. By 1925 Mussolini had become a dictator, known as *il Duce* (the Leader). The Fascists seized control of all aspects of Italian life,

▷ Oswald Mosley set up the British Union of Fascists after a visit to Italy in 1932. At public meetings his supporters, known as "the Blackshirts," often behaved very violently.

△ *The Italian Fascist leader Benito Mussolini was a great friend and ally of Germany's Adolf Hitler. Italy joined forces with Hitler in World War II.*

Propaganda posters

The Spanish government produced anti-Fascist propaganda posters like this during the civil war. They urged the people to oppose the Fascist leaders.

such as newspapers, industry and education, and ensured that anyone who disagreed with Fascist points of view was imprisoned or murdered. Mussolini continued to rule until he was overthrown during World War II, in 1943.

General Franco

In Spain, a bitter civil war broke out in 1936. Supported by the Fascist *Falangé* group, the army rose against the Spanish government. The rebels, known as Nationalists, were led by General Francisco Franco. People who fought to save the government were known as Republicans. This war attracted much interest, as Fascist countries such as Germany and Italy supported the Nationalists. The Republicans were backed by the Soviet Union, and many people from other European countries went to Spain to fight for the Republican cause. The Nationalist forces eventually seized power in 1939, and General Franco became dictator of Spain, ruling until his death in 1975.

△ *Adolf Hitler was known as der Führer (the Leader). He believed that Germany needed strong leadership to solve its problems, which he blamed on communists and Jews. He put himself in charge of all Germany's armed forces.*

The Nazis

In the early 1930s, the Nazi party rose to power in Germany, led by Adolf Hitler. Humiliated by the terms of the peace treaties at the end of World War I, and suffering the effects of the Great Depression, the German people responded to Hitler's promises of national recovery. Hitler became chancellor of Germany in 1933, and began removing all opposition to the Nazi party. He set up a secret police force, banned opposing political parties, and started to persecute minority groups in the German population, such as gypsies and Jews. He also planned to take back land lost at the end of World War I. These actions led to the outbreak of World War II.

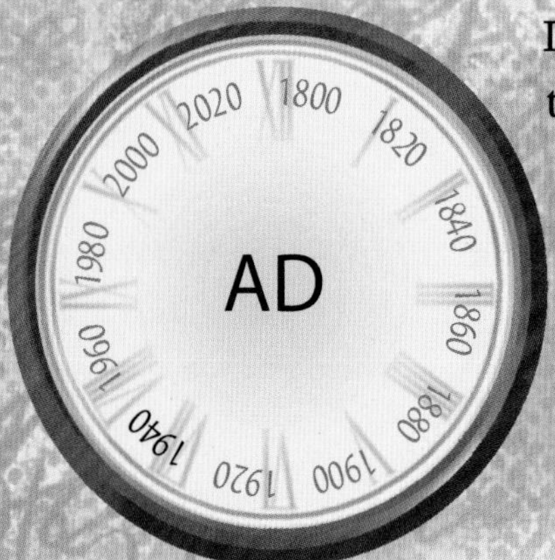

In March 1939, the German leader Adolf Hitler threatened to invade Poland. Hitler had already shown the seriousness of his intentions by taking over Austria (in 1938) and Czechoslovakia (in 1939).

World War II

Both Great Britain and France gave guarantees to help Poland if it was attacked. So when Hitler invaded Poland on September 1, 1939 Britain and France were forced to declare war on Germany.

September: Hitler invades Poland.	1939
September: Britain and France declare war on Germany.	1939
USSR invades Poland.	1939
April–May: Germany occupies Denmark, Norway, Belgium, the Netherlands.	1940
Germany occupies France. June: Allies evacuate troops from Dunkerque.	1940
June: French sign armistice with Germany. July: Battle of Britain starts.	1940
Italians invade Egypt. Allies fight to prevent Axis control of Suez Canal.	1940
Hitler sends General Erwin Rommel to North Africa.	1941
Germany invades USSR. December: Japanese attack on Pearl Harbor.	1941

Under Hitler's leadership, Germany had been well prepared for war. During 1939 and 1940, German troops scored victories in Poland, Denmark, Norway, Belgium, the Netherlands, and France. Before the war started, Hitler had signed a "non-aggression pact" with the Soviet Union, both sides promising not to attack the other. As German troops swept across Europe, Soviet troops attacked Estonia, Latvia, Lithuania, and Finland.

The Battle of Britain

The Allied forces of Britain and France became trapped by the rapid German invasion. The majority of the British army was saved in 1940 by a desperate evacuation from the French port of Dunkerque. In June 1940, the French signed a truce with Germany and Britain stood alone against the German military machine.

Italy joined the war, siding with the Germans, in June 1940, and Hitler made plans to invade Britain. However, first he needed to gain control of the skies. The Battle of

△ *Allied troops wait on a beach at Dunkerque, in northern France, in June 1940. A rescue fleet of naval ships, fishing boats, yachts, and ferries sailed across the English Channel from England to carry them back to safety. In all, the evacuation rescued more than 300,000 soldiers, who had become trapped by the German army.*

△ *Winston Churchill was Britain's wartime leader from May 1940 until just before the war ended. Here he is seen making his famous "V for victory" sign.*

Battle of Britain

The Battle of Britain was the world's first major air battle. The British fighter planes were able to shoot down many of the long-range German bomber aircraft, shown here.

Britain began in July 1940 between the German airforce, the Luftwaffe, and Britain's Royal Air Force (RAF). The Luftwaffe bombed RAF bases, as well as British towns and cities. The nightly air raids that took place in the autumn and winter of 1940–1941 are known as the Blitz. However, by May 1941 the RAF had gained the upper hand, and Hitler gave up the attempt to bomb Britain into submission although air raids continued throughout the war.

Pearl Harbor

Meanwhile, the fighting spread beyond Europe. In Africa, Italian troops invaded Egypt, threatening the Suez Canal. The canal was a vital link to the oilfields of the Middle East, so Allied troops were sent to defend Egypt. Germany also made a surprise attack on the Soviet Union, going back on the promises made in the non-aggression pact. The German invasion, in June 1941, took the Russian leader Stalin by surprise.

In December 1941 there was another surprise attack, this time by the Japanese airforce on the U.S. navy base at Pearl Harbor in Hawaii. Although the attack crippled the U.S. Navy in the Pacific Ocean, it also drew the U.S. into the war. The United States and the Allies declared war on Japan on December 8, 1941. Japan joined Germany and Italy to form the Axis alliance.

"... we shall fight on the seas and oceans, we shall fight with growing confidence ... in the air, we shall defend our island, whatever the cost may be ...
WINSTON CHURCHILL, JUNE 4, 1940"

△ *A standard World War II helmet. About 17 million soldiers, from both the Allies and the Axis countries, were killed during the war.*

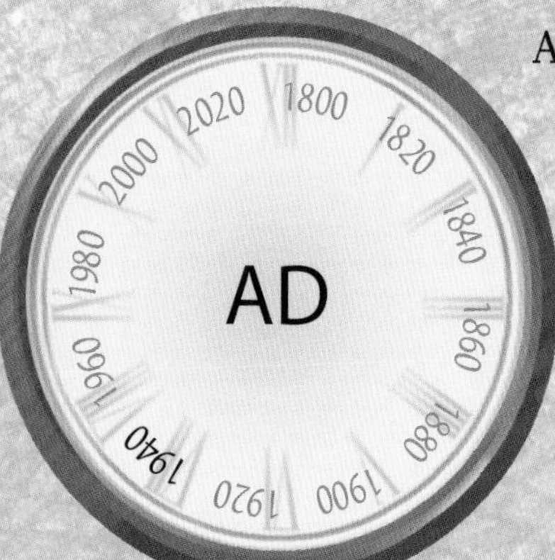

After the attack at Pearl Harbor in 1941, World War II became a truly global war. In Africa, the Allies succeeded in defeating the Italians, only to be pushed back once again by Axis troops under the command of Hitler's General Rommel.

A Global War

The turning point came at the battle of el-Alamein in October 1942, when Allied forces, under Lieutenant-General Montgomery, forced the Axis troops to retreat. The Axis forces eventually surrendered in North Africa in May 1943.

April: Doolittle Raid on Tokyo, Japan. May: battle of Coral Sea. — 1942

June: Midway Island. August: Guadalcanal. October: battle of el-Alamein. — 1942

February: siege of Stalingrad ends with Axis surrender. — 1943

May: Axis forces surrender in North Africa. — 1943

July: battle of Kursk. September: Allied troops land in Italy. — 1943

June: D-Day invasion along Normandy coast, northern France. — 1943

June: battle of the Philippine Sea. December: battle of the Bulge. — 1944

May 7: German surrender. May 8: Victory in Europe. September: Japanese surrender. — 1945

War in the Pacific

After Pearl Harbor, Japanese forces quickly took control of much of Southeast Asia, including Singapore, Burma (Myanmar), and the Philippines. The Japanese then advanced across the Pacific toward Australia and the Hawaiian Islands. From 1942 to 1945 the Allies continued to drive the Japanese out of their newly captured territories.

△ On the morning of June 6, 1944, thousands of Allied troops went ashore along the coast of Normandy in northern France in what became known as the D-Day landings.

▷ *Japan's surprise attack on Pearl Harbor, on December 7, 1941, brought the Americans into the war. During the summer of 1942, U.S. forces successfully halted the Japanese advance at the battles of Midway Island, Guadalcanal and Coral Sea.*

The Soviet Union

By November 1941 German troops had advanced almost as far as Moscow. The bitter Russian winter and the Soviet army combined to drive them back. The German forces advanced into Soviet territory again, reaching the city of Stalingrad (now Volgograd). The Soviet army finally defeated the Germans in a fierce battle in the city.

△ *Charles de Gaulle was the leader of the French troops, known as the Free French, who had escaped occupied France. After the war he became one of France's most powerful presidents ever.*

The end of the war

In June 1944, Allied leaders decided that it was time to attack Germany itself. Under the overall command of General Eisenhower, Allied troops landed in Normandy and advanced across France. Meanwhile, Soviet troops moved across eastern Europe.

In April 1945, as Soviet troops surrounded Berlin, Hitler committed suicide. The German surrender came on May 7, and the Allies declared May 8 V-E (Victory in Europe) day. However, in the Far East the war was not over. President Harry S. Truman, decided to use a secret weapon developed by British and American scientists – the atomic bomb. On August 6th and 9th, 1945, two atomic bombs were dropped on the Japanese cities of Hiroshima and Nagasaki. The Japanese surrendered on September 2.

The Holocaust

In places such as Belsen and Auschwitz, the Nazis had set up concentration camps, where millions of Jews were imprisoned and murdered. An estimated six million Jews died in these camps in World War II, an event known as the Holocaust.

△ *By 1945 many Allied cities, as well as the country's factories and railways, were in complete ruins as a result of the German bombing campaign.*

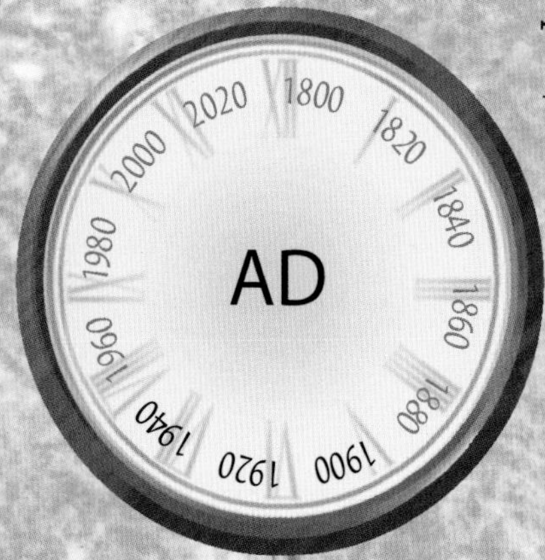

Technological advances in the machines and weapons of war were rapid during the 20th century. During World War I, inventions included the tank and the fighter aircraft. At sea, one of the major advances in military marine technology happened before the war, with the building of the battleship *Dreadnought*.

New War Technology

Britain launches new type of battleship called Dreadnought.	1906
Trench warfare claims thousands of lives in World War I.	1914–1918
Tanks used effectively for first time at battle of Cambrai.	1917
World War II involves much of the world in a global war.	1939–1945
German troops use blitzkrieg tactics to invade Allied countries.	1940
U.S. sets up secret nuclear research project.	1942
First atomic bomb exploded in New Mexico.	1945
Atomic bombs dropped on Hiroshima and Nagasaki in Japan.	1945

During World War II, the Germans used a new type of warfare, known as *Blitzkrieg* (lightning war). In the United States, scientists developed the atomic bomb, which was used to bring the war against Japan to its catastrophic end.

Trench warfare and tanks

By the end of 1914, the Allies and the Germans had reached a stalemate on the Western Front. Both sides dug defensive trenches to protect their troops. The trenches of the opposing sides were separated by a desolate and deserted strip called "no man's land."

From 1914 to 1918, both sides attacked the other's trenches with little success. Thousands of men were killed in these pointless offensives. Tanks were developed to move across rough ground and through the barbed wire that protected trenches, while giving the soldiers inside some protection.

△ The line of trenches dug by the forces of the Allies and the Central Powers in World War I eventually ran from the English Channel almost to Switzerland. The nearest trench to the enemy was known as the "front line," but complex trench systems extended many miles back from this.

War in the air

At the beginning of World War I, aircraft were used for reconnaissance, to collect information about enemy positions and movements. Enemy aircraft began to exchange gunfire in the air, and soon machine guns were mounted onto aircraft. Flying "aces" such as the German

△ *Both the British and the French armies experimented with tanks during World War I. These armored vehicles were first used to effect at the battle of Cambrai in 1917.*

Atomic bombs

The first atomic bomb was exploded in an experiment in New Mexico, in July 1945. A month later, atomic bombs were used to end the war. The bombs dropped on Japan killed about 130,000 people. Many more suffered radiation and burn injuries.

Red Baron, Erich von Richthoffen, fought daring one-to-one air battles in the skies.

Aircraft played a vital role in World War II. The German airforce, the *Luftwaffe*, tried to bomb Britain into submission in 1940. But in the Battle of Britain the British RAF finally gained control of the skies. The German *Luftwaffe* also dropped bombs immediately before overwhelming tank and infantry attacks on the ground.

War at sea

Although the battle of Jutland was the only major sea battle of World War I, control of the seas was vital. The Germans made very effective use of submarines, known as U-boats, to launch torpedo attacks on enemy shipping.

By World War II, massive ships called aircraft carriers could transport air power across the seas. The Japanese attack on Pearl Harbor in 1941 destroyed many U.S. battleships, but the U.S. Navy played a decisive part in the many Pacific battles of the war. The Atlantic Ocean was also a war zone, with German U-boats attacking ships to try to prevent supplies reaching Britain. However, the convoy system, in which ships traveled in groups protected by warships, helped to reduce the number of ships lost to U-boat attacks.

"Men marched asleep. Many had lost their boots
But limped on, blood-shod. All went lame; all blind;
Drunk with fatigue;...
DULCE ET DECORUM EST, WILFRED OWEN

Owen fought in World War I and wrote poems about his experiences."

△ *The introduction of machine guns made World War I more deadly than earlier wars. From the trenches, machine guns easily wiped out large numbers of attacking soldiers.*

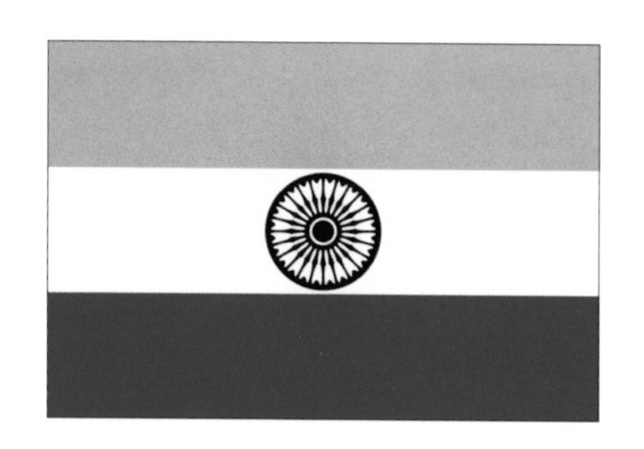

World War II came to an end in 1945 after the Allies dropped two atomic bombs on the Japanese cities of Hiroshima and Nagasaki. To try to prevent such a conflict happening again, the victorious Allies set up the United Nations, an international peacekeeping organization.

Global Politics

At the end of the war, the Union of Soviet Socialist Republics (USSR) and the United States emerged as the world's two "superpowers." Differences between the USSR and its communist allies, including China, on the one hand, and the U.S. and other non-communist countries on the other, soon led to the start of the "Cold War." Although neither superpower fought the other directly, both sides began to build up large supplies of nuclear weapons.

Communism

After World War II, the USSR moved quickly to extend communist power in Eastern Europe. By 1948 there were communist governments in Albania, Bulgaria, Czechoslovakia, Hungary, Poland, Romania, and

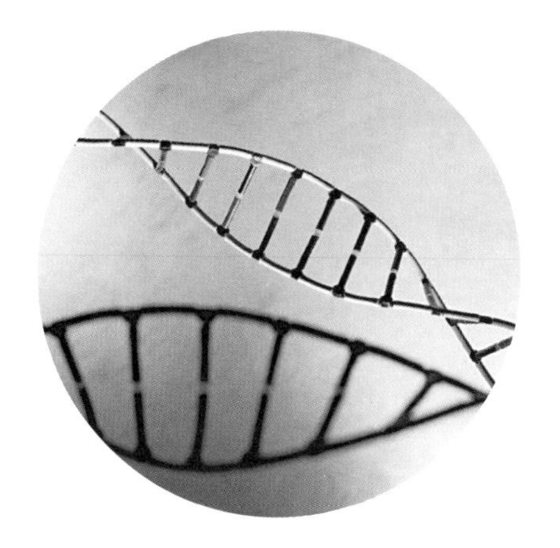

Yugoslavia. However, in the 1960s there was a major split in the communist world when China and the USSR ceased friendly relations. In China, Mao Zedong returned to power in 1966, launching the Cultural Revolution which lasted until his death in 1976. In the USSR, dissatisfaction with the communist system led to reforms in the 1980s and the eventual collapse of communism in Eastern Europe in 1989 and 1990. The USSR itself finally broke up into independent republics in 1991.

Independence

Another major change in the years after World War II was the break up of the colonial empires held by European nations. The independence of India in 1947 marked the beginning of this process. However, independence was often achieved with bloodshed. In India, the partition (division) of the country led to violence between Hindus and Muslims. In Africa, there were violent clashes in many places, and independence sometimes resulted in civil war. In South Africa, the white minority government enforced a racist policy called apartheid (meaning separateness), which tried to keep black and white people apart.

Into the 21st century

Many people's lives have been transformed by the communications revolution in the 21st century. Radio, television, and the Internet have made the world a smaller place, with people communicating more easily and quickly than ever before. Many people now realize that some of the major challenges of the 21st century cannot be faced by countries separately. Environmental matters such as pollution and climate change affect people all over the planet, and countries need to work together to find solutions. Global awareness is one of the main challenges facing the world in the 21st century.

After the revolution of 1911, the last Chinese emperor, the six-year-old Pu Yi, gave up his throne. The revolutionaries named Sun Yat-sen as temporary leader of the new republic, but in 1912 a soldier named Yuan Shikai became president.

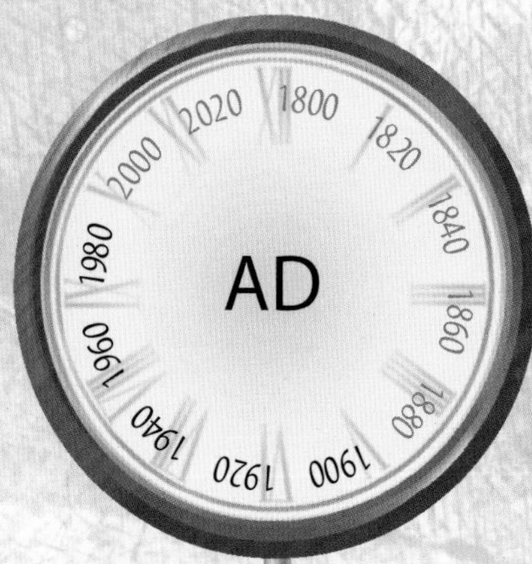

Communist China

Yuan quickly tried to seize more power, attempting to make himself emperor, but he died in 1916. Meanwhile, Sun Yat-sen had become leader of the Chinese National People's Party (also known as the Kuomintang), with support from many warlords (military leaders) in the south of China.

Last Chinese emperor gives up throne.	1911
Chinese Communist Party founded.	1921
Nationalist government established in China.	1928
Communists set up a rival government in the south.	1931
Mao Zedong leads "Long March."	1934–1935
War with Japan.	1937–1945
Nationalists flee to Taiwan. Mao Zedong proclaims the birth of the People's Republic of China.	1949
Period of "Five-Year Plan."	1953–1957
Start of the "Great Leap Forward."	1958
Mao launches Cultural Revolution.	1966
Death of Mao.	1976

For some years the Nationalist Party worked closely with Chinese communists, aided by the USSR who wanted to promote communism in China and help the revolution. The Communist Party attracted many students, including a young Mao Zedong. Mao and other students did much to spread communism among the rural poor of China.

Sun Yat-sen died in 1925, and the nationalists' new leader was Chiang Kai-Shek. A military leader, he led a campaign to defeat rebellious warlords in the north. He also crushed communist power in the cities, establishing a nationalist government in 1928.

The Long March

In 1931, the communists set up a rival government in the south. Chiang Kai-Shek sent his armies to crush the communists once and for all. The communists were forced to flee and

▷ ***A crowd gathers during the Long March of 1934–1935. About 100,000 communists made the difficult 6,000-mile journey northwards.***

△ *A poster from modern China. Wall posters have been used to provide information for many years. This one tries to encourage people to adopt a modern attitude.*

Mao Zedong

During the Cultural Revolution, Mao and his supporters accused many people of failing to follow communist ideals. Students and young people formed groups of "Red Guards" in support of Mao.

△ *Millions of Chinese would read the ideas of Mao printed in what became known as Mao's "Little Red Book."*

moved north on a journey, known as the "Long March," led by Mao Zedong. Pursued by nationalist soldiers, thousands of marchers died.

War with Japan

The nationalist government also had to cope with constant threats from Japan, and in 1937 the Japanese invaded China. In World War II, China fought with the Allies against Japan. After the end of the war, and Japan's defeat, in 1945, China again descended into civil war. Aided by popular support, the communists gradually gained the upper hand. In 1949, Chiang Kai-shek and his supporters fled to Taiwan, and Mao proclaimed China the People's Republic of China.

China under Mao

After years of civil war, much of China was in ruins. Mao Zedong set about reforming the country according to communist ideals. Land was seized from landowners and divided up among the peasants. In Mao's "Five-Year Plan" (1953–1957) new roads and railways were built, industry was boosted, and health and education were improved. However, the main challenge was to produce enough food to feed China's huge population. The "Great Leap Forward," which started in 1958, was a second plan to improve agricultural and industrial output. But the plan failed and Mao retired in 1959.

In the early years of the People's Republic, China was supported by the USSR. However, China became increasingly critical of the USSR, particularly of its relations with the West, and the two countries ceased friendly relations in the 1960s. In 1966, Mao Zedong came back to power in China, launching the Cultural Revolution to promote communist ideals. Many teachers were forced to go and work on the land, and schools and universities closed down. Thousands of people were killed or sent into exile for criticizing Mao or questioning his policies. The Cultural Revolution eventually came to an end in 1976, when Mao died.

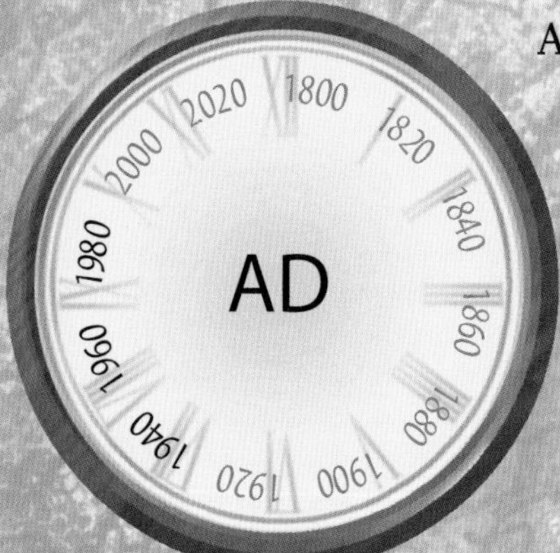

At the end of World War I in 1918, many people were determined that there should never again be such terrible slaughter and bloodshed. An international association called the League of Nations was formed by the leading nations involved in the war.

The United Nations

First UN conference held in San Francisco. UN Charter signed.	1945
UN approves plan to set up Jewish state of Israel.	1947
UN approves Universal Declaration of Human Rights.	1948
UN negotiates between U.S. and USSR during Cuban missile crisis.	1962
UN arranges ceasefire to end Six-Day War in Middle East.	1967
UN arranges ceasefire between Iran and Iraq.	1988
UN sends peacekeeping force to Croatia.	1992
UN peacekeeping troops sent to Bosnia.	1993

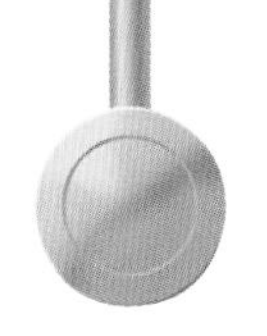

The League of Nations aimed to maintain peace between countries. However, although US president Woodrow Wilson was a driving force behind the League's formation, he was unable to persuade Congress to join it. In the years to come this proved to be a serious weakness.

Founding the United Nations

The League began to fall apart in the 1930s when several member states challenged its authority. After the outbreak of war in 1939 the League of Nations ceased to exist, but there were moves to establish a new organization to replace it. In 1941 President Franklin D. Roosevelt, and the British prime minister, Winston Churchill, signed the Atlantic Charter. It pledged to respect people's rights to choose their government, to

△ *An aid worker in an African feeding station. The UN's World Food Program gives emergency food aid and other kinds of assistance to help developing countries.*

▷ Representatives from 26 countries signed a document known as the "Declaration of United Nations" on January 1, 1942. An additional 21 countries later signed the same declaration. It was the first time the term "United Nations" had been used.

maintain peace, and to live without fear or want, as well as promoted disarmament and economic prosperity.

In 1944, representatives from the United States, the USSR, China, and Great Britain attended a series of meetings in the U.S. They drew up the basis for an international peacekeeping organization. The first conference of the United Nations (UN) was held in San Francisco in 1945, and the UN Charter was signed in October of that year.

△ *An Ethiopian soldier of one of the UN's many peacekeeping forces. In recent years the UN has sent its peacekeeping forces into trouble spots such as southern Lebanon, Bosnia, Rwanda and East Timor.*

The aims of the UN

Peace and security are the most important aims of the UN. Since 1945, the UN has helped to negotiate peace deals and has provided peacekeeping forces. The Cold War between the United States and the USSR caused many tensions in the UN, but since the break up of the Soviet Union, cooperation between member countries has increased.

As well as working for peace, the UN also has many other branches, called agencies, that deal with worldwide problems. Some of these agencies provide aid for people in need, such as refugees. Others are concerned with health matters, living and working conditions, and human rights.

The General Assembly

Delegates from the UN's member countries meet in the Auditorium of the General Assembly Building in New York. The General Assembly chooses the members of the UN's other main bodies, and decides how much money each member country should contribute to UN funds. It also controls the amount of money given to each UN organization.

△ The official flag of the United Nations consists of a map of the world circled by two olive branches. Olive branches are a symbol of peace.

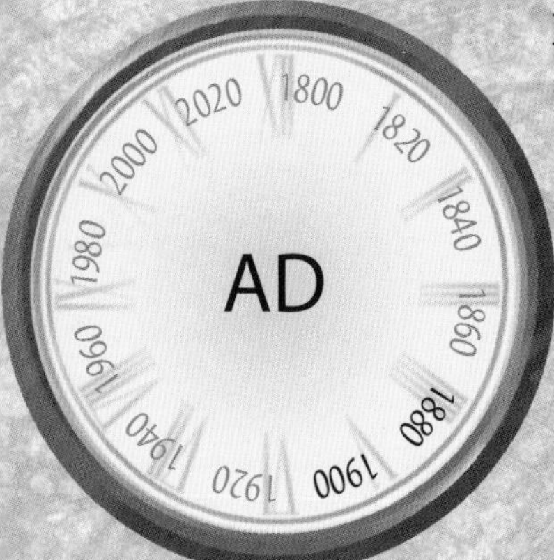

During the 1800s, India became Britain's most important colonial territory. India provided Britain with cheap raw materials, particularly cotton, for its developing industries, as well as a large market for Britain's manufactured goods.

India's Independence

Many Indian citizens wanted independence from British rule and a chance to build up industry and wealth in India itself. In 1885, the Indian National Congress was founded. At first this political party worked for moderate reform, but after 1917 it became more extreme, campaigning for home rule.

Indian National Congress founded.	1885
Mohandas Gandhi becomes leader of Indian National Congress.	1920
Gandhi launches campaign of non-violence against British.	1920
Gandhi leads "Salt March."	1930
World War II.	1939–1945
Gandhi imprisoned by the British.	1942
Two regions in northeast and northwest India become Muslim state of Pakistan.	1947
India becomes independent.	1947
Hindu assassin murders Gandhi.	1948

During World War I, many Indian troops fought bravely in Europe for the Allies. In return, Indian citizens expected more participation in their own government.The first Government of India Act in 1919 made some reforms, but British officials kept most of the power. Protest meetings were held throughout India. In Amritsar, British troops fired on a crowd protesting against the reforms. Over 350 people were killed and at least 1,000 injured.

Amritsar and after

The Amritsar massacre inspired many Indian citizens to step up the fight for independence. In 1920, a lawyer named Mohandas Gandhi became leader of the Indian National Congress. He started a campaign of non-violent disobedience against British rule. It included the refusal to pay taxes and to attend British courts and schools.

In the early 1920s Gandhi organized a boycott of British manufactured goods in

△ Many of the demonstrations by Indian people seeking independence ended in violence. The British soldiers were often ruthless in their treatment of the demonstrators.

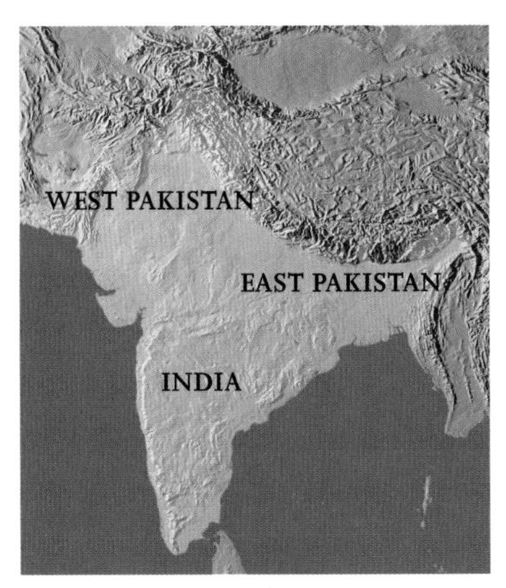

△ *India gained her independence from Britain on August 15, 1947. The previous day, two regions in northeast and northwest India had become the Muslim state of Pakistan.*

Gandhi

Mohandas Gandhi was known as Mahatma Gandhi (*mahatma* means "great soul"). In 1930 he led the famous "Salt March" to the coast in protest at a law forcing people to buy heavily taxed salt. Gandhi was assassinated in 1948, at the end of India's long struggle for independence.

India. Gandhi himself was imprisoned several times, where he continued his policy of non-cooperation by going on a hunger strike.

Partition and independence

By the end of World War II, it was clear that Britain could no longer ignore the demands of Indian nationalists. Negotiations were complicated by the demands of Muslims in India. Although the majority of India's population were Hindu, there were also a large number of Muslims. The leader of the Muslim League, Mohammed Ali Jinnah, demanded the creation of a separate state, called Pakistan, in regions of India where Muslims were in the majority.

Violence broke out between Hindus and Muslims, and Indians and British leaders eventually agreed to partition (divide) India into the two states of Hindu India and Muslim Pakistan. After partition took place in August 1947, millions of Hindus and Muslims fled from their homes, yet the violence continued. As people tried to move to their new homes hundreds of thousands of people were killed.

The first prime minister of independent India was Jawaharlal Nehru. Mohammed Ali Jinnah became the first governor-general of Pakistan.

> Oh, East is East, and West is West, and never the twain shall meet, Till Earth and Sky stand presently at God's great Judgment Seat …
>
> *THE BALLAD OF EAST AND WEST*, RUDYARD KIPLING
>
> *Kipling was an English poet and writer who was born in Bombay, India.*

△ *In the center of India's flag is an ancient symbol of a wheel. It is known as the Dharma Chakra, which means the "Wheel of Law."*

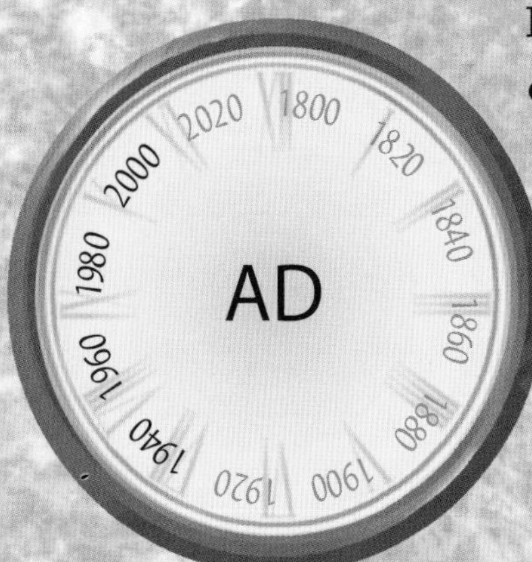

By the early 20th century, Jewish people lived all over the world, particularly in European countries, the United States and Russia. In the late 1800s, some Jews had established a movement known as Zionism.

The Middle East

The Zionists called for Jews to return to the area around Jerusalem, which they considered their spiritual homeland. Since Jerusalem was part of the Turkish (Ottoman) Empire, the area was inhabited largely by Arabs. As more Jews arrived in the area of Palestine, tension grew between the Arab inhabitants and Jewish immigrants.

Founding of the state of Israel. Arab League declares war.	1948
End of first Arab-Israeli war.	1949
Egypt takes over control of Suez Canal. Second Arab-Israeli war.	1956
Palestinian Liberation Organization (PLO) is founded.	1964
Six-Day War ends in victory for Israel.	1967
Yom Kippur War.	1973
Israel and Egypt sign peace agreements at Camp David.	1978
Israel and PLO sign agreement to work to end differences.	1993

In 1917, the British government issued the Balfour Declaration, offering support for a Jewish homeland in Palestine. At the end of the war the Turkish Empire was broken up, and the League of Nations gave Britain a mandate (authority) to rule Palestine. Jewish immigration increased rapidly in the 1930s as thousands of Jews fled Nazi persecution in Europe.

The creation of Israel

At the end of World War II, the demand for a Jewish state in Palestine grew. In 1947, the United Nations took over responsibility for Palestine, dividing it into an Arab state and a Jewish state. The Jews agreed to this

△ Civil war between Christians and Muslims broke out in Lebanon in 1975. Fighting continued during the late 1970s and 1980s, causing extensive damage in the city of Beirut.

▷ *Arab refugees from the Six-Day War between Israel and its Arab neighbors, which took place in May 1967. As a result of the war, Israel gained control of large areas of land in the Sinai Peninsula as well as the city of Jerusalem and Syria's Golan Heights.*

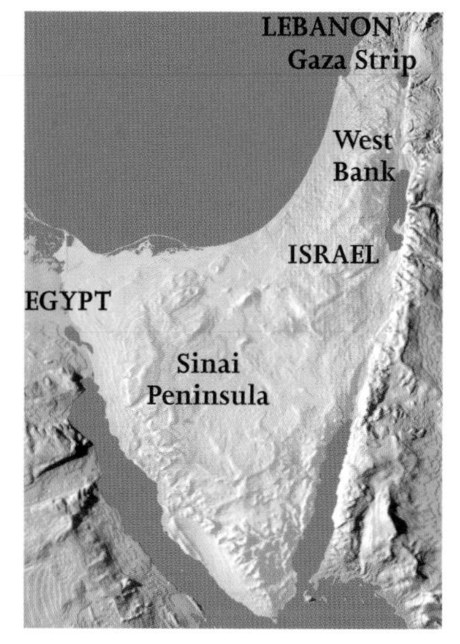

△ *Israel has borders with Lebanon and Syria, Jordan, and Egypt. In 1967 Israel occupied the territories of the Gaza Strip and the West Bank, home to over one million Palestinian Arabs, and the Sinai Peninsula.*

plan, but the Arabs did not. The state of Israel came into being on May 14, 1948. It was immediately attacked by Arab armies from Egypt, Syria, Lebanon, Iraq, and Transjordan (Jordan) – known collectively as the Arab League. By 1949, Israel had defeated the Arab League and added land to its own territory.

War in the Middle East

The Jewish immigrants who flocked to Israel needed land in the new state, so the Palestinian Arabs were pushed into smaller areas. Some fled to live as refugees in neighboring Arab states. Others demanded a separate state of their own. This led to the founding of the Palestinian Liberation Organization (PLO) in the 1960s.

Relations between Israel and its Arab neighbors continued to be extremely difficult. In the Six-Day War, Israel destroyed much of the Arab air forces and gained extra territories. Israel also gained the upper hand in the Yom Kippur War in 1973.

In 1993, Israel and the PLO recognized each other, and the first steps were taken toward Palestinian self-rule. The negotiations continue into the 21st century, although tensions between Israelis and Arabs continue to disrupt the peace process.

The United States and the Middle East

Since 1979, a number of peace treaties between Israel and its Arab neighbors have been signed, mostly under the watchful eye of the United States. President Bill Clinton (left) played a key role in the negotiations that led to the Oslo Accords, which were signed by the Israeli prime minster Yitzhak Rabin and PLO leader Yasir Arafat. They laid out the terms of a peace settlement between Israel and the PLO.

△ *The Damascus Gate, one of several historic gates leading into the old city of Jerusalem. Since the Six-Day War of 1967 both East Jerusalem and West Jerusalem have been under Israeli control. The city is a sacred place for Jews, Muslims, and Christians alike.*

After World War II, European nations found themselves coming under increasing pressure to dismantle their colonial empires. In some places independence was achieved peacefully. In others, the move to independence was marked by violence and bloodshed.

New Nations

- **1948** Ceylon (present-day Sri Lanka) and Burma (Myanmar) independent.
- **1957** Ghana is first African British colony to become independent.
- **1957** Start of war in Vietnam (lasted until 1976).
- **1962** Algeria becomes independent from France.
- **1963** Kenya becomes independent from Britain.
- **1965** Rhodesia (present-day Zimbabwe) declares independence from Britain.
- **1975** Angola and Mozambique independent from Portugal.
- **1991** End of apartheid in South Africa.
- **1994** Nelson Mandela becomes first black president of South Africa.

The independence of India marked the start of the break up of the British Empire. In 1948 Ceylon (present-day Sri Lanka) and Burma (Myanmar) became independent. In Africa, the first British colony to achieve independence was the Gold Coast, which became Ghana in March 1957.

The Commonwealth

After independence many former British colonies became members of the Commonwealth of Nations. This is an association of states that maintain friendly links and cooperation with each other. They accept the

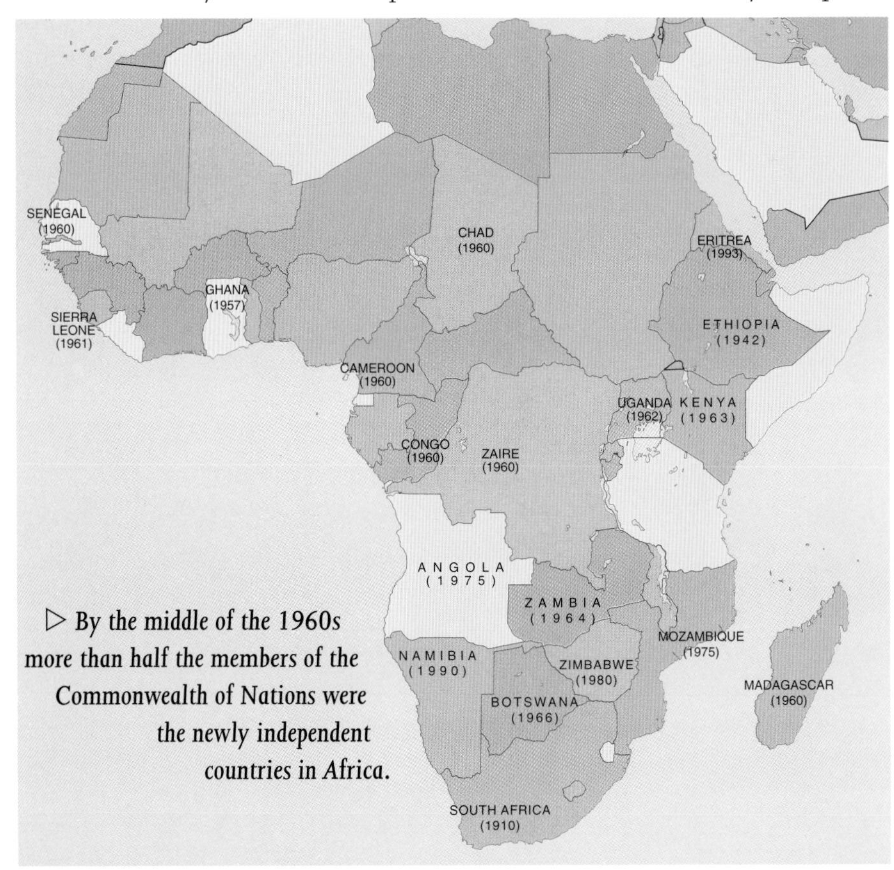

▷ By the middle of the 1960s more than half the members of the Commonwealth of Nations were the newly independent countries in Africa.

△ *Kwame Nkrumah became prime minister of the Gold Coast in 1952 and led the country to its independence, as Ghana, in 1957. He was president of Ghana from 1960 to 1966.*

△ *South Africa's policy of apartheid involved separating black and white people in public places such as parks, beaches, cinemas, and sports stadiums.*

△ *The flag of the Commonwealth of Nations, which includes Britain and more than 50 independent nations that were at one time British colonies.*

Vietnam War

The Vietnam War between North and South Vietnam lasted from 1957 until 1976. In 1965 the United States was drawn into the war to support South Vietnam. This is a statue of remembrance in Washington D.C.

British monarch as the symbolic head of the Commonwealth. It now consists of more than 50 independent nations.

Conflict in Africa

Although the process of independence was orderly and peaceful in many British colonies, in some places there was conflict. This happened particularly in places where there were white settlers, who were often unwilling to give up or share power. In Kenya, this situation led to guerrilla warfare between British forces and a group called the Mau Mau. After years of violence, Kenya finally became independent in 1963. In British Central Africa, the white minority seized power and declared its independence in 1965, as Rhodesia. Years of struggle resulted in victory for the black majority in 1980, and the country's name was changed to Zimbabwe.

In South Africa, the white government adopted a racist policy called "apartheid" (separateness), which denied black people the right to vote and segregated (divided) them from white people in housing, public places, transport, and schools. This policy came to an end in 1991, and Nelson Mandela was elected as the first black president of South Africa in 1994.

The French Empire

The dismantling of the French Empire led to conflict in many areas. This was because the French saw their colonies as part of "Greater France" and were unwilling to let them go completely. There were also many French settlers in places such as Algeria, where independence was granted in 1962 after fighting that claimed over 250,000 lives. In Southeast Asia, the French fought the Indochina War against the Communist Vietminh. The outcome was French defeat in 1954, and the division of Vietnam into two nations.

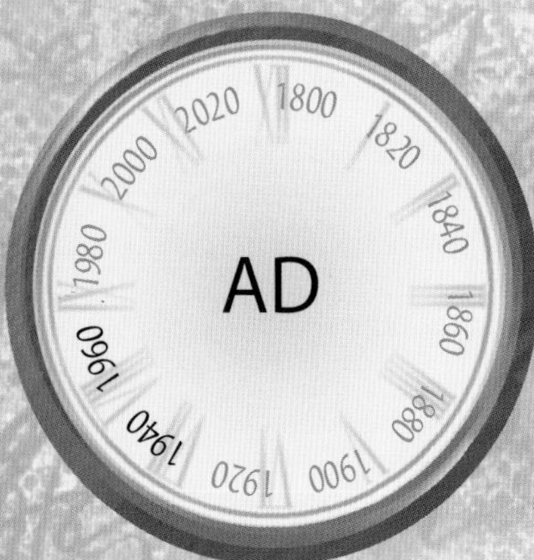

After World War II, the United States and the USSR emerged as the two main powers in the world – known as "superpowers." Although they had fought together to defeat Nazi Germany, differences between the two superpowers soon led to the start of the "Cold War."

The Cold War

Blockade of Berlin and Berlin airlift.	1948–1949
NATO founded.	1949
Korean War. North Korea is backed by the Soviets, South Korea by the U.S.	1950–1953
Warsaw Pact founded among countries of Eastern Europe.	1955
Split between USSR and China.	1960
Berlin Wall constructed.	1961
The Cuban missile crisis.	1962
USA becomes involved in Vietnam War, defending South Vietnam against invasion from the communist north.	1964

The Cold War was a political war between the USSR and its communist allies, and the U.S. and other non-communist countries. It did not involve fighting, although there was a threat of military action on several occasions.

The Iron Curtain

After the end of World War II, the Soviet leader Joseph Stalin quickly placed communist governments in the eastern European countries that Soviet troops had liberated from the Germans. The British prime minister, Winston Churchill, claimed that an "iron curtain" fell across Europe as the USSR tightened its control of eastern Europe. The Soviets wanted to protect themselves against any future threat from Germany, and to spread communism. By 1948, there were communist governments in Albania, Bulgaria, Czechoslovakia, Hungary, Poland, Romania, and Yugolsavia.

△ During the blockade of the German capital Berlin by Soviet forces in 1948–1949, aircraft flew essential supplies to the people trapped inside the city for 11 months. This operation became known as the Berlin airlift.

The Berlin airlift

At the end of World War II, Germany itself was divided into four zones, controlled by the United States, France, Great Britain, and the USSR. The capital of Germany, Berlin, lay within the Soviet zone, but was itself divided. In 1948, the United States,

△ *In 1945 the three Allied leaders – Winston Churchill, Franklin D. Roosevelt, and Joseph Stalin – met at Yalta to discuss the problems facing postwar Europe.*

J. F. Kennedy

John Fitzgerald Kennedy was president from 1961 until he was assassinated in 1963. During his presidency the Berlin Wall was built, dividing the city in two and stopping East Germans escaping communist rule.

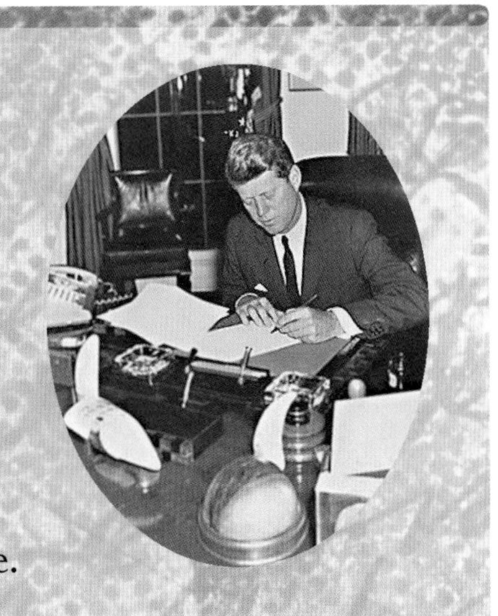

France, and Great Britain (the Western Allies) joined their zones to form the German Federal Republic (West Germany). The USSR replied by blockading the parts of Berlin controlled by the Western Allies. In May 1949 the USSR ended the blockade, and the Soviet-controlled part of Germany became the German Democratic Republic (East Germany).

The Cuban crisis

In 1949, the Western Allies formed the North Atlantic Treaty Organization (NATO) for defense against the communist presence in Europe. In the same year, the USSR exploded its first atomic bomb. With both superpowers holding nuclear weapons, fear and mistrust between the two sides increased.

The Soviets constructed a wall across Berlin in 1961, separating East from West in the city. In 1962, the Cuban missile crisis erupted when the U.S. discovered that the USSR was building missile sites on the island of Cuba in the Caribbean. The two superpowers came to the brink of war before the USSR agreed to withdraw the weapons. Although the two superpowers never became involved in direct warfare, both sides became involved in wars elsewhere in the world; the United States fought communism, and the USSR helped communist fighters.

> "All free men, wherever they may live, are citizens of Berlin, and, therefore, as a free man, I take pride in the words 'Ich bin ein Berliner'.
> J. F. KENNEDY, WEST BERLIN, JUNE 26, 1963"

△ *The discovery of Soviet-built missile sites on Cuba alarmed the United States. The missile sites were within range to launch an attack by nuclear weapons on American cities.*

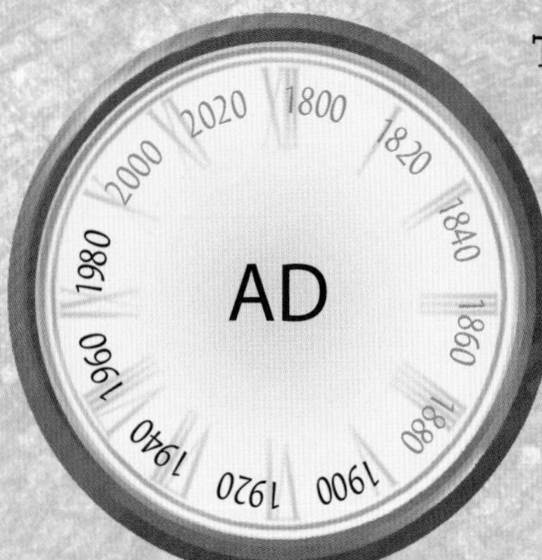

The 20th century saw an explosion in communications technology. The first radio broadcast was made almost at the beginning of the century, when Reginald A. Fessenden transmitted music and words in 1906.

Communications

By the end of the 20th century, people were communicating by electronic mail (e-mail) across the world at the touch of a computer key. This revolution, together with faster and improved methods of travel, has changed life for almost everyone around the globe.

First radio broadcast by Reginald A. Fessenden.	1906
John Logie Baird develops first successful television set.	1926
British Broadcasting Company (BBC) makes first television broadcasts in UK.	1936
Color television begins in USA.	1953
First communications satellite, Echo 1, launched.	1960
First TV programs transmitted by U.S. Telstar satellite.	1962
Transatlantic phone calls transmitted by Earlybird satellite.	1965
First microprocessor is built.	1972
First personal computer developed.	1975

Radio and television

By the 1920s, radio provided a major form of entertainment for many people around the world. Then, in 1926, a Scottish engineer named John Logie Baird developed the first successful television set. The earliest black and white TV broadcasts were made by the British Broadcasting Company (BBC) in 1936. The first major event to be broadcast internationally was the coronation of Queen Elizabeth II in 1953. Color television began in the U.S. in the same year.

Satellites

In order to send radio signals around the Earth, scientists developed communications satellites. These satellites are sent up into orbit around the Earth. Signals are beamed up to the satellite from a transmitter on the Earth's surface. The satellite then retransmits the signal back down to a receiver on the ground. The transmitter and receiver are often thousands of miles apart. The first communications

▷ ***A broadcast is transmitted from an early TV studio. At the outset, the United States moved quickly ahead of other countries in the field of TV broadcasting.***

△ *The CN Tower in Toronto, Canada is a communications and observation tower. When completed in 1976, it was the world's tallest free-standing structure.*

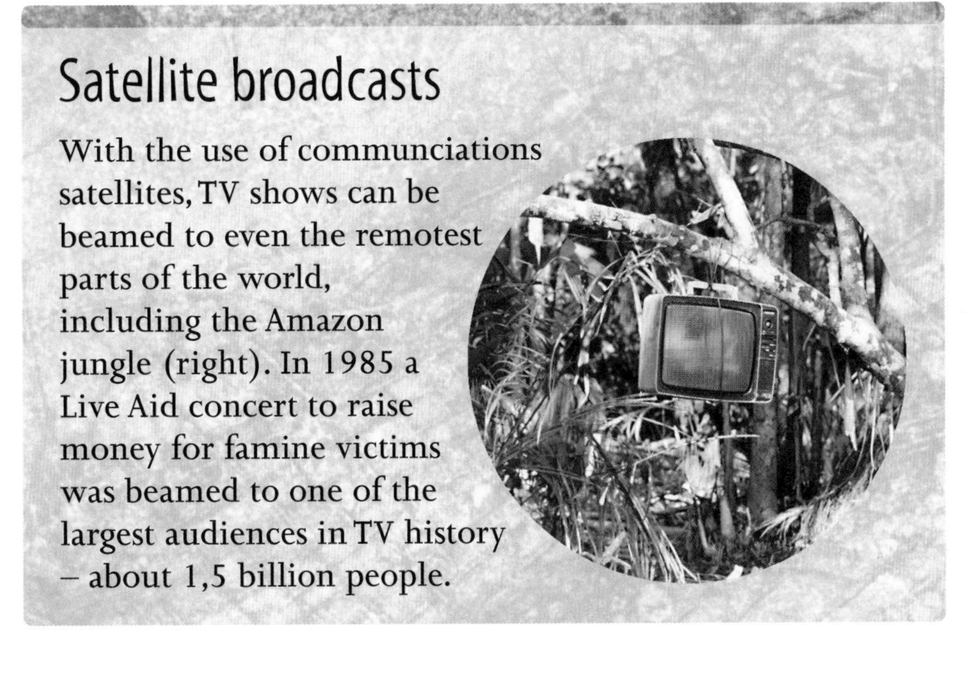

Satellite broadcasts

With the use of communciations satellites, TV shows can be beamed to even the remotest parts of the world, including the Amazon jungle (right). In 1985 a Live Aid concert to raise money for famine victims was beamed to one of the largest audiences in TV history – about 1,5 billion people.

satellite used to relay telephone messages across the globe was called *Echo 1*, launched in 1960. The first TV programs were transmitted by the U.S. *Telstar* satellite in 1962.

△ *Today, hundreds of satellites are in orbit around the Earth, relaying radio and TV programs, and telephone calls around the world.*

Computers

The earliest computers were calculating machines, dating back to the 1600s. However, the first electronic computers were developed in the 1930s and 1940s. These machines were huge and took a long time to program. As computers became smaller and faster, more and more people began to use them. In the past 30 years, computers have revolutionized almost every aspect of modern-day life. Today, many people own a home computer, on which they use the Internet to look up information, to play games, and even to do their shopping, as well as to send and receive e-mail.

Latest technology

Some of the latest advances in technology use light instead of waves to transmit information. Glass fiberoptic cables carry information in the form of laser beams. Many TV stations now relay programs by cable, which goes directly into people's homes. These cables can also carry telephone calls as well as computer data.

◁ *At home, people use e-mail to communicate with their family and friends. Messages can be sent to the other side of the world in a few seconds.*

△ *Since the early 1990s the mobile phone has proved to be an increasingly popular means of communication.*

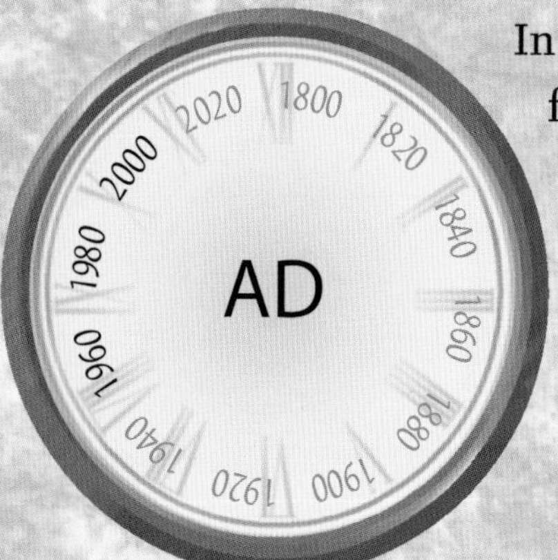

In the early 1960s, China and the USSR had ceased friendly relations, causing a split between the two main powers in the communist world. In the late 1960s and 1970s, divisions between the two world superpowers – the USSR and the U.S. – began to ease.

Communism Collapses

A growing dissatisfaction with communism and Soviet rule began to take hold in many Eastern European countries. Meanwhile, economic growth in the countries of Western Europe meant that the United States was not quite the dominating force it had been immediately after World War II.

- *First Strategic Arms Limitation Talks (SALT).* — 1972
- *Second SALT agreement. Soviet invasion of Afghanistan.* — 1979
- *Ronald Reagan becomes U.S. president and launches "Starwars" defense project.* — 1981
- *Solidarity trade union banned in Poland.* — 1982
- *Mikhail Gorbachev becomes Soviet leader and starts reforms.* — 1985
- *Reagan and Gorbachev sign treaty to ban medium-range nuclear missiles.* — 1987
- *Berlin Wall is dismantled. Free elections in Poland.* — 1989
- *Collapse of communism in Eastern Europe. East and West Germany unified.* — 1990
- *Gorbachev resigns and USSR is abolished.* — 1991

Nuclear weapons

A major area of tension between the U.S. and the USSR was the arms race. This was a race to build up increasing numbers of weapons, particularly nuclear missiles. In 1969, the first of a series of meetings were held between the two sides to limit the production of nuclear weapons. These meetings, known as the Strategic Arms Limitation Talks (SALT), saw the signing of two agreements in 1972 and 1979. But the Soviet invasion of Afghanistan in 1979 caused a worsening of relations, and the U.S. continued to make defense plans in case of a Soviet attack.

In 1985, Mikhail Gorbachev became the new leader of the USSR. His program of reforms reduced the tension between the two superpowers. In 1989, Soviet troops withdrew from Afghanistan.

▷ **The Berlin Wall had separated communist East Berlin from non-communist West Berlin for almost 30 years. In November 1989 the people of Berlin demolished the hated wall.**

△ Mikhail Gorbachev introduced a program of political, social, and economic reforms, called perestroika. His policy of glasnost (openness) gave Soviet people more freedom of expression.

Communist rule

With the end of communist rule in the USSR, many of the symbols of communism, for example statues of former leaders such as Lenin (right), were quickly dismantled.

Eastern Europe

As the policies of *perestroika* (economic reforms) and *glasnost* (openness) took effect in the USSR, governments in the Eastern European countries began to lose control. The collapse of communism in Eastern Europe took place in 1989 and 1990. Borders were opened, allowing people to travel freely for the first time since the 1940s. Free elections were held in Poland in 1989, and in 1990 in Czechoslovakia, Hungary, East Germany, Romania, and Bulgaria. East and West Germany were unified in October 1990.

△ President Ronald Reagan was a keen supporter of Mikhail Gorbachev's program of reform in the USSR. In 1987 the two leaders signed an agreement to dismantle many kinds of nuclear weapons.

The end of the USSR

Gorbachev accepted the fall of the communist regimes in Eastern Europe. However, there were many states within the USSR who also wanted freedom from Soviet central government. Inspired by the collapse of communism in Eastern Europe, the Baltic state of Lithuania declared its independence in 1990. Other states called for separation and more self-government. In 1991 there was a coup – an attempt to overthrow Gorbachev's government. The coup failed, but Gorbachev was forced to resign. His resignation on December 25, 1991 signaled both the end of the USSR and the Cold War. The former states of the USSR became 15 independent republics.

△ In Poland, the free trade union Solidarity was banned in 1982. Criticism of the communist regime was suppressed in Eastern European countries under Soviet rule.

> It is not what they built. It is what they knocked down. It is not the houses. It is the spaces between the houses. It is not the streets that exist. It is the streets that no longer exist.
>
> *A GERMAN REQUIEM*, JAMES FENTON
>
> *Fenton worked as a journalist in Germany, as well as Cambodia.*

As we enter the 21st century, people are becoming increasingly concerned with issues that affect the world as a whole. This is due partly to the improved speed of communication, and the ease of travel between one place and another.

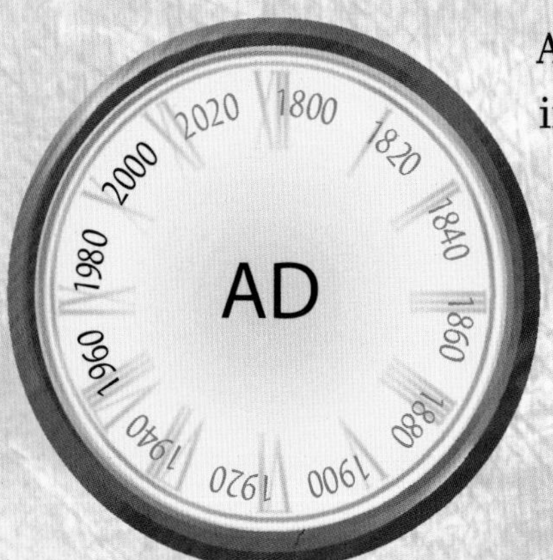

Global Concerns

You can jump on a plane and be on the other side of the world within 24 hours. When you log onto the Internet, you can find out about almost any subject, or chat with people thousands of miles away. One of the major issues of the late 20th century was concern for our environment. Up until the 1960s, most people were unaware of, or unconcerned about, human impact on the Earth.

Rachel Carson publishes Silent Spring.	1962
Environmental organization Greenpeace is founded.	1971
U.S. government bans pesticide DDT.	1972
Explosion and fire at Chernobyl nuclear reactor, Ukraine.	1986
Hole discovered in ozone layer above Antarctic.	1987
Earth Summit in Rio de Janeiro, Brazil.	1992

Harming the environment

In 1962, an American scientist called Rachel Carson published a book called *Silent Spring*, in which she wrote about the harmful effects of pesticides on animal life. In the 1970s, organizations such as Friends of the Earth and Greenpeace began to campaign on many environmental issues. These included the destruction of the rainforests in places such as South America and Southeast Asia, the dumping of toxic nuclear

▷ *Violent tropical storms called hurricanes leave behind a trail of damage and destruction. Scientists are concerned that changes in the world's climate as a result of global warming may increase the number of these devastating storms.*

△ Greenpeace campaigns on many environmental issues around the world. It opposes whaling, using its boats to try and separate whaling ships from their catch.

waste, the effects of pollution, and protection for endangered species such as the whale and the rhinoceros.

Today, a major issue that will affect everybody on the planet in some way is global warming. When we burn fossil fuels such as oil (from which petrol and diesel are made) and coal, carbon dioxide gas is given off into the atmosphere. With the massive increase in the use of fossil fuels in our homes, factories and vehicles, the amount of carbon dioxide in the atmosphere has increased, too. Carbon dioxide is just one of the gases, known as greenhouse gases, that trap the Sun's heat around the Earth. Scientists know that more heat is being trapped inside our atmosphere and that the Earth is becoming warmer. What they cannot be sure about is the effect of global warming in the future.

△ The international symbol for radiation. It is used to warn people that they are close to radioactive material.

Agenda 21

One thing is certain, however: global warming and other environmental issues are problems that have to be tackled by nations all over the world working together. In 1992, the representatives of countries from around the world met at the Earth Summit in Rio de Janeiro, Brazil. The result was Agenda 21 – an agenda for action in the 21st century.

Agenda 21 covers environmental issues such as pollution and wildlife protection, but it also covers human issues which are just as important for life in the 21st century. There is a huge imbalance between life in the rich countries of the developed world and the poorer nations of the developing world. Global planning to improve this imbalance is one of the main challenges facing the world in the 21st century.

△ In tropical areas, rainforests are cut down to clear the land for farming. Trees are vital to life on Earth because they take in carbon dioxide gas and release oxygen.

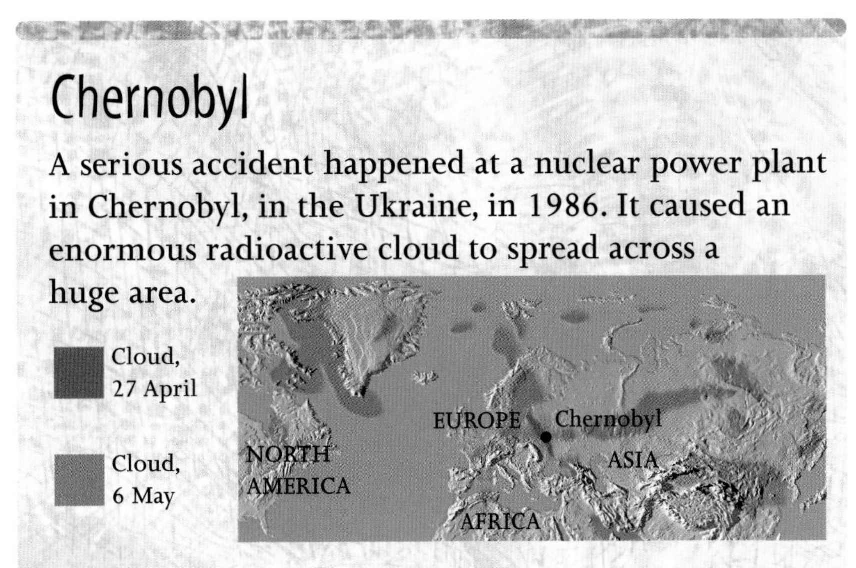

Chernobyl
A serious accident happened at a nuclear power plant in Chernobyl, in the Ukraine, in 1986. It caused an enormous radioactive cloud to spread across a huge area.
Cloud, 27 April
Cloud, 6 May
EUROPE
Chernobyl
NORTH AMERICA
ASIA
AFRICA

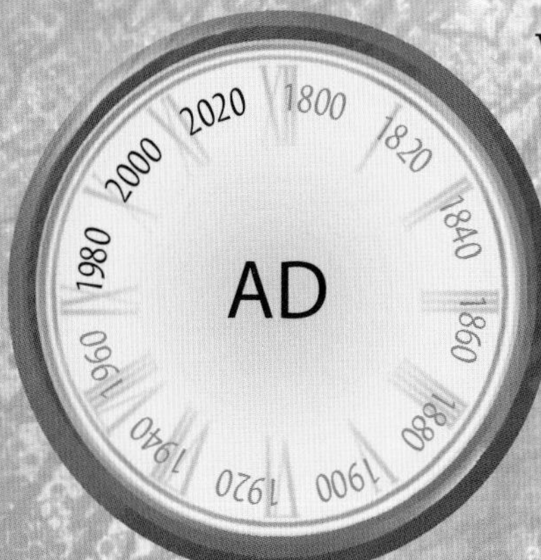

What will life be like during the 21st century? At the dawn of the 20th century, the airplane was still only a dream, motor cars were rare and wonderful things, and movies had only just started.

Tomorrow's World

By the end of the 20th century, all of these things were taken for granted by the vast majority of the world's population. What advances can we expect throughout the 21st century?

1980s	Doctors identify previously unknown disease called AIDS.
1981	Start of NASA's space shuttle program.
1990	Start of Human Genome Project (HGP) – due for completion in 2003.
1990	Launch of Hubble Space Telescope.
1993–2004	Russia, U.S., and others join together to work on International Space Station.
1999	Campaign to end Third World debt gains in importance.
1999	UN estimates 11.5 million refugees in the world.

Medicine

Major advances in medicine in the 20th century included the discovery of penicillin in 1928, the development of a vaccine against polio in the 1950s, and the first heart transplant in 1957. Nevertheless, despite all that modern medicine can offer, new diseases can and do occur. In the early 1980s, doctors identified a previously unknown disease that attacks the body's immune system. Called AIDS (acquired immuno-deficiency syndrome), this disease is caused by the human immuno-deficiency virus (HIV) and thus far it has claimed millions of lives.

One of the most exciting areas of medicine for the 21st century is the Human Genome Project (HGP). This project, which is due to be completed in 2003, is an international project, involving 18 countries.

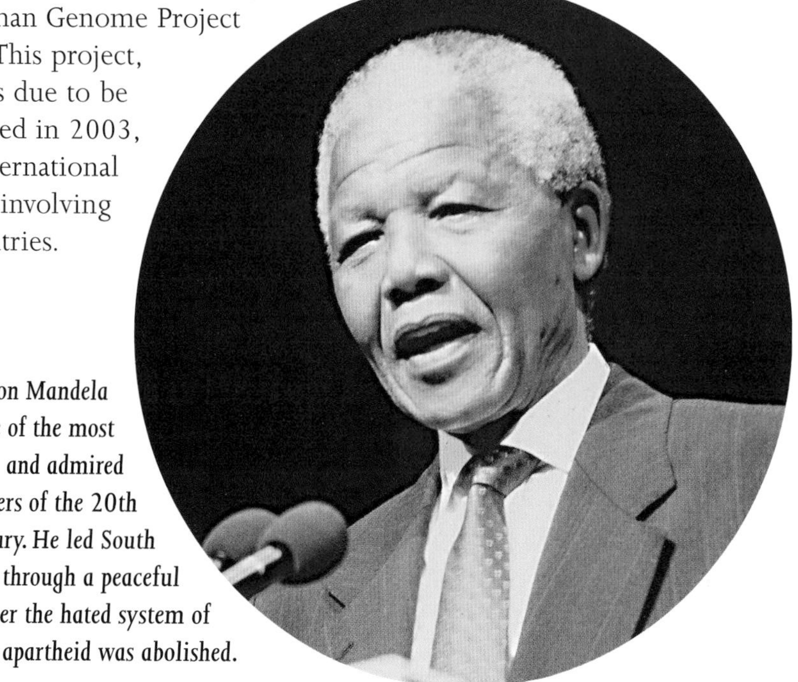

▷ *Nelson Mandela was one of the most respected and admired leaders of the 20th century. He led South Africa through a peaceful change after the hated system of apartheid was abolished.*

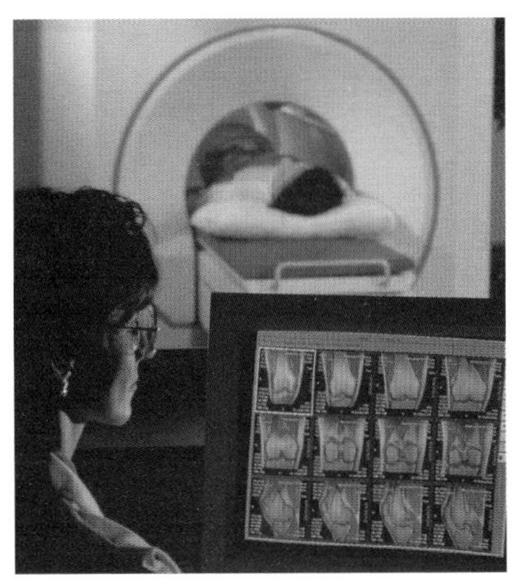

△ A medical worker examines the pictures from an MRI (magnetic resonance imaging) scanner. It takes pictures in slices through the body.

International Space Station

The ISS should be complete in 2004. It will be used for research in medicine and other fields and is seen as a step toward future space exploration.

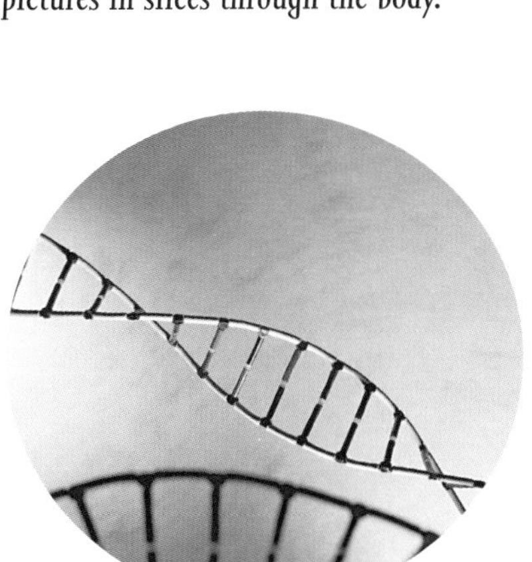

△ A model of DNA (deoxyribonucleic acid), the genetic material that is found in the cells of living things.

Its aim is to discover all of the 100,000 genes (the human genome) in the human body by studying the DNA. As a result of this, and other research, genetics will play an increasingly important role in the diagnosis, monitoring, and treatment of diseases in the 21st century.

Space technology

The Space Race started during the Cold War, when the USSR and the U.S. competed with each other to put the first person into space and onto the moon. Today, the former superpowers are working together on projects in space. The International Space Station (ISS), the largest scientific project in history, involves a total of sixteen nations.

War and peacekeeping

Everyone hopes that the 21st century will not see a repeat of the terrible slaughter of World War I and World War II. With the United Nations in place as an international organization for peace and security, nations will hopefully go to the negotiating table rather than to war. Even as the 21st century began, there was conflict in many places, for example Chechnya, in Russia. Elsewhere, peace-keeping forces maintain a fragile peace in places such as Kosovo.

△ UN peacekeeping soldiers in Bosnia. In the future, it is likely that troops will find themselves increasingly called upon to act as peacekeepers in places where there are conflicts and tension.

Third World debt

Without doubt, a key issue in the 21st century will be the contrast between rich and poor countries. One of the main problems is "Third World debt." In the 1970s, many developing countries borrowed money from richer countries. Banks charged interest on the loan repayments. Many developing nations now struggle to repay even just the interest. There is a growing campaign to cancel Third World debt, so that developing countries can put more resources into areas such as education and health.

Kings of England

Saxons

Egbert AD 827–839
Ethelwulf AD 839–858
Ethelbald AD 858–860
Ethelbert AD 860–866
Ethelred I AD 866–871
Alfred the Great AD 871–899
Edward the Elder AD 899–924
Athelstan AD 924–939
Edmund AD 939–946
Edred AD 946–955
Edwy AD 955–959
Edgar AD 959–975
Edward the Martyr AD 975–978
Ethelred II the Unready AD 978–1016
Edmund Ironside AD 1016

Danes

Canute AD 1016–1035
Harold I Harefoot AD 1035–1040
Hardicanute AD 1040–1042

Saxons

Edward the Confessor AD 1042–1066
Harold II AD 1066

Normans

William I the Conqueror AD 1066–1087
William I AD 1087–1100

Rulers of Scotland

Malcolm II AD 1005–1034
Duncan I AD 1034–1040
Macbeth AD 1040–1057
Malcolm III Canmore AD 1057–1093
Donald Bane AD 1093–1094
Duncan II AD 1094
Donald Bane (restored) AD 1094–1097
Edgar AD 1097–1107

Notable Roman Emperors

Augustus (Octavian) 27 BC–AD 14
Tiberius AD 14–37
Caligula AD 37–41
Claudius AD 41–54
Nero AD 54–68
Vespasian AD 69–79
Trajan AD 98–117
Hadrian AD 117–138
Marcus Aurelius AD 161–180
Diocletian AD 284–305
Constantine I AD 308–337
Theodosius I the Great AD 378–395

Chinese Dynasties

Hsia before 2200 BC–1500 BC
Shang 1500–1122 BC
Zhou 1122–256 BC
Qin 221–207 BC
Han 202 BC to AD 220 (with break)
Three kingdoms and six dynasties AD 220–581
Sui AD 581–618
Tang AD 618–907
Five dynasties and ten kingdoms AD 907–960
Sung (ruled part of China only) AD 960–1279

Famous Battles of Ancient Times

Marathon Greeks beat Persians 490 BC
Salamis (sea) Greeks beat Persians 480 BC
Gaugamela (Arbela) Greeks beat Persians 331 BC
Cannae Hannibal beat Romans 216 BC
Actium (sea) Octavian beat Antony 31 BC
Teutoberg Forest Germans beat Romans 9 BC
Tours (Poitiers) Franks beat Muslims AD 732
Lechfeld Emperor Otto beat Magyars AD 955
Hastings Normans beat English AD 1066
Manzikert Turks beat Byzantines AD 1071

The Seven Wonders of the Ancient World

The Pyramids of Egypt
Built in the 2000s BC, and the only Wonder to survive. The largest is the Great Pyramid of Cheops, 482 ft high.

Hanging Gardens of Babylon
Terraced gardens built about 600 BC by King Nebuchadnezzar for his wife.

Statue of Zeus at Olympia
Carved by Phidias in the 400s BC. Made of ivory and gold, it stood on the site of the first Olympic Games.

Temple of Artemis at Ephesus
Marble temple with over 100 columns, which took about 120 years to build. Destroyed in AD 262.

Mausoleum at Halicarnassus
Huge tomb in memory of King Mausolus of Caria in Asia Minor, who died in 353 BC.

Colossus of Rhodes
Statue of the sun god Apollo, about 118 ft high, at the harbour entrance. Destroyed by earthquake in 224 BC.

Pharos of Alexandria.
Lighthouse built about 270 BC in harbor of Alexandria, Egypt. Destroyed by earthquake in AD 1375.

Kings and Queens of England, 1100 to 2000

Henry I	1100–1135
Stephen	1135–1154
Henry II	1154–1189
Richard I	1189–1199
John	1199–1216
Henry III	1216–1272
Edward I	1272–1307
Edward II	1307–1327
Edward III	1327–1377
Richard II	1377–1399
Henry IV	1399–1413
Henry V	1413–1422
Henry VI	1422–1461
Edward IV	1461–1483
Henry VI (restored)	1470–1471
Edward V	1483
Richard III	1483–1485
Henry VII	1485–1509
Henry VIII	1509–1547
Edward VI	1547–1553
Mary	1553–1558
Elizabeth I	1558–1603
James I	1603–1625
Charles I	1625–1649
Commonwealth and Cromwell's Protectorate	1649–1660
Charles II	1660–1685
James II	1685–1688
William III and Mary	1689–1702
Anne	1702–1714
George I	1714–1727
George II	1727–1760
George III	1760–1820
George IV	1820–1830
William IV	1830–1837
Victoria	1837–1901
Edward VII	1901–1910
George V	1910–1936
Edward VIII (abdicated)	1936
George VI	1936–1952
Elizabeth II	1952–today

Presidents of the USA

George Washington	1789–1797
John Adams	1797–1801
Thomas Jefferson	1801–1809
James Madison	1809–1817
James Monroe	1817–1825
John Quincy Adams	1825–1829
Andrew Jackson	1829–1837
Martin Van Buren	1837–1841
William Henry Harrison	1841
John Tyler	1841–1845
James Polk	1845–1849
Zachary Taylor	1849–1850
Millard Fillmore	1850–1853
Franklin Pierce	1853–1857
James Buchanan	1857–1861
Abraham Lincoln	1861–1865
Andrew Johnson	1865–1869
Ulysses S. Grant	1869–1877
Rutherford B. Hayes	1877–1881
James Abram Garfield	1881
Chester A. Arthur	1881–1885
Grover Cleveland	1885–1889
Benjamin Harrison	1889–1893
Grover Cleveland	1893–1897
William McKinley	1897–1901
Theodore Roosevelt	1901–1909
William H. Taft	1909–1913
Woodrow Wilson	1913–1921
Warren G. Harding	1921–1923
Calvin Coolidge	1923–1929
Herbert C. Hoover	1929–1933
Franklin D. Roosevelt	1933–1945
Harry S. Truman	1945–1953
Dwight D. Eisenhower	1953–1961
John F. Kennedy	1961–1963
Lyndon B. Johnson	1963–1969
Richard Nixon	1969–1974
Gerald Ford	1974–1977
Jimmy Carter	1977–1981
Ronald Reagan	1981–1989
George Bush	1989–1993
Bill Clinton	1993–2000
George W. Bush	2001–present

Dynasties of China 1279 to present

Yuan (Mongol)	1279–1368
Ming	1368–1644
Qing (Manchu)	1644–1912
Establishment of the Republic of China	1912
China united under Nationalist Government	1928
Establishment of People's Republic of China	1949

Battles of World War I

August 25–30, 1914
Battle of Tannenberg
September 6–9, 1914
First Battle of the Marne
February 1915
Battle of the Masurian Lakes
April–December 1915
Gallipoli campaign
February–July 1916 Battle of Verdun
May 31 – June 1, 1916
Battle of Jutland (naval battle)
July 1 –November 1916
Battle of the Somme
April 9 – May 17, 1917
Battle of Vimy Ridge
April 16 – May 1917
Nivelle Offensive
July 31 – November 10, 1917 Battle of Passchendaele
July 15 – August 6, 1918
Second Battle of the Marne

Battles of World War II

July 1940–May 1941
Battle of Britain and Blitz
June 1941 Operation Barbarossa
German invasion of Russia
September 1941–January 1944
Siege of Leningrad
December 7, 1941
Japanese attack on U.S. Pacific Fleet at Pearl Harbor
May 1942 Battle of the Coral Sea
June 1942 Battle of Midway
August 1942–February 1943 Battle of Stalingrad
October 1942 Battle of El Alamein
July 1943 Battle of Kursk
June 6, 1944 D–Day landings
October 23–6, 1944 Battle of Leyte Gulf
December 1944 Battle of the Bulge

Index